OUTLANDER
Cocktails

THE OFFICIAL DRINKS GUIDE
Inspired by the Series

James Shy Freeman

Food recipes by Rebecca Marsters ✦ *Foreword by Diana Gabaldon*

RANDOM HOUSE WORLDS
NEW YORK

Contents

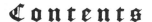

FOREWORD

I started drinking because of *Outlander*.

During my childhood, my mother didn't drink at all, and my father drank only beer, while watching sports on TV. He once gave me a sip of his Budweiser—I was two—and I never willingly drank alcohol again (barring a polite glass of Blue Nun when invited to dinner with friends) until I was taken to a German winery many years later and given *Federweißer*—a milky white new wine, very mild (haha) and delicious with *Zwiebelkuchen*.

The stuff was served in ten-ounce water glasses. Six glasses later, I nearly died of alcohol poisoning on the way home. (No, I wasn't driving, thank God . . .) By concentrating fiercely on taking each breath as we slalomed down the long, pitch-black, and winding road back from the vineyard, I survived to resume a cautious experimentation with the fruits of the vine some years later.

Having eventually discovered—around age thirty-five—that all wine didn't taste like Blue Nun (or the ghastly sour Chablis that seemed to be the only other white wine sold in US supermarkets at the time), I gradually developed the ability to drink wine with dinner (at a restaurant) two or three times a year.

Then I wrote *Outlander,* a novel set in Scotland. In both the book and the country, people frequently make and consume whisky. Given my limited experiments with exotic alcohols, it never occurred to me to actually try the stuff myself. But when my third book, *Voyager,* was published in 1994, a nice fan who had come to a book signing presented me with a large bottle of Glenrothes single malt Scotch.

This sat ornamentally on my desk for several months. One night I was staring at it (sitting and staring at things is an integral part of my creative process) when it occurred to me that perhaps I should at least *taste* the stuff, the better to write about it. (This philosophy of experimentation in the pursuit of one's craft leads to a lot of Really Interesting Tax Deductions, I tell you . . .)

So I did. And gradually sipped my way through the whole bottle, not merely becoming used to the taste of whisky, but actually enjoying the stuff.

As we began to travel to Scotland whenever an opportunity offered, people started generously giving me more whisky. I also toured several distilleries (for research purposes, of course, but it's only polite to buy something on the way out . . .) and began to be able to tell one whisky from another.

(Lagavulin, if you're wondering, is my favorite. Also very fond of Oban, Talisker, Highland Park [18], and . . . well, the only one I've tasted so far that I didn't care for was Ardbeg, which—apparently on purpose—smells and tastes strongly of seaweed and dead fish.)

Then we began to make a bit more money, and we started drinking wine at home now and then, no longer just for special occasions. And on one of our Scotland trips we toured the Edradour whisky distillery.

Distilleries give out free samples because it's the most effective way of marketing their product. I appreciate the wisdom of this philosophy, and since my third book I've always handed out free samples, in the form of scenes from the book of the moment, posted online. (My first beloved editor used to say to me, "These *have* to be word-of-mouth books, because they're too weird to describe to anybody." This Is True . . .)

So we bought a bottle of Edradour.

We also encountered the Whisky Heritage Centre (now relabeled as "The Scotch Whisky Experience") at the top of the Royal Mile. Six-hundred-plus single malt Scotch whiskies (and quite a few good blends) on the shelves, and a Very Well-Stocked tasting room downstairs.

Luckily we walked back to the hotel. We took the Edradour home to Arizona and sipped it with slow appreciation.

Our palates now fully mature (along with the rest of us), we cautiously broadened our experimentation.

Now, my husband (who modestly refuses to be named here) is a Maker. He makes things, he builds things, he fixes things, he makes things better. That's what he does.

A bottle of wine, no matter how good, offers little scope to a man of active imagination and a bone-deep inclination to tinker. So it was no surprise that he should eventually venture into the varied world of cocktails and mixed drinks.

My own habit is an unimaginative (but enjoyable) glass of Champagne before dinner, sipped while admiring his experiments with Herbstura (which is what you get when you mix Angostura bitters with Herbsaint—which, in turn, is what one uses in lieu of absinthe, if you prefer not to go blind after the third glass) and the vast range of rums, tequilas, flavored gins, orgeat (pronounced "OR-zhat"; it's basically chilled and sweetened dilute almond milk), and entertaining liqueurs like Ancho Reyes, Aperol, and the very poetically named Velvet Falernum, etc.

My main contribution to the fruits of his creative energy is to applaud and grow mint with which to garnish some of the drinks he creates (see "The Pterodactyl," on the next page), but I thought those of you who like cocktails might appreciate a couple of his creations.

Slàinte mhath!

—DIANA GABALDON

Scottsdale, Arizona ✦ July 2023

Diana's Mimosa

Have one after you are done writing for the day. Then have another. Champagne flutes are small.

¾ ounce LUXARDO SANGUE MORLACCO CHERRY LIQUEUR (see note)

1½ ounces PINK GRAPEFRUIT JUICE (ideally chilled)

2 LUXARDO ORIGINALE MARASCHINO CHERRIES

CHAMPAGNE (your favorite and/or the best you can afford) for topping

Add the Sangue Morlacco, the grapefruit juice, and the cherries to a champagne flute. Top with Champagne.

NOTE: *The Luxardo Sangue Morlacco liqueur is not the Luxardo cherry stuff that comes in the bottles with the basketry.*

The Pterodactyl

Another rum-plus-Campari cocktail that we know of is the Jungle Bird, which has pineapple juice and is sort of girlie. In contrast, the Pterodactyl is a nice stiff drink, manly and seafaring. Pterodactyls eat jungle birds as snacks.

Or so we thought. On our latest visit to the Museum of Natural History in New York, we learned that the wingspan of the pterodactyl was only about twelve inches. The really big pterosaurs were guys like Quetzalcoatlus *and* Pteranodon. *But everybody has heard of a pterodactyl and knows it as being gnarly, so we stand by the name.*

1½ ounces LIGHTLY AGED BLENDED RUM (see note)

¾ ounce CAMPARI

½ ounce FRESHLY SQUEEZED LIME JUICE

1 teaspoon SIMPLE SYRUP (page 188)

2 to 3 dashes ANGOSTURA BITTERS

DEHYDRATED LIME WHEEL for garnish

Add all the ingredients to a cocktail shaker. Add ice and shake until chilled. Strain into a chilled cocktail glass. Garnish with the dehydrated lime wheel. If you want, you can splash in a bit more simple syrup to taste.

NOTE: *Good rum choices would be Appleton Estate Signature or Mount Gay Eclipse. Pierre Ferrand would be a good choice for dry curaçao, but of course any good example from the Cointreau/curaçao/Triple Sec family will do as well.*

Rum, Sodomy, and the Lash

In 1913 Winston Churchill, then First Lord of the Admiralty of the British Royal Navy, was in the midst of a very contentious strategy meeting with his admirals. At one point in the argument, one of them accused Churchill of "having impugned the traditions of the Royal Navy," to which he replied, "And what are they? They are rum, sodomy, and the lash."

In this cocktail (working backward), the Lash is represented by the bite of the Ancho Reyes. The Herbsaint in the Herbstura bitters is absinthe-ish, and absinthe historically has been associated with debauchery, so I guess the Herbsaint will be our Sodomy. Rum is represented by . . . the rum.

1½ ounces AGED BLENDED RUM
(see note)

1 ounce DRY CURAÇAO

¼ teaspoon ANCHO REYES CHILE
LIQUEUR

½ ounce FRESHLY SQUEEZED LIME JUICE

1 teaspoon SIMPLE SYRUP, plus more
(optional) as needed (page 188)

2 to 3 dashes HERBSTURA BITTERS
(see note)

MINT SPRIG and DEHYDRATED
LIME WHEEL for garnish

Add all the ingredients to a cocktail shaker. Add ice and shake until chilled. Strain into a chilled cocktail glass. Garnish with the mint and the dehydrated lime wheel. If you want, you can splash in a bit more simple syrup to taste.

NOTES: *Good rum choices would be Doorly's XO or Appleton Estate Reserve. We like Pierre Ferrand dry curaçao, but of course any good example from the Cointreau/curaçao/Triple Sec family will do as well.*

The Herbstura bitters you can make yourself. It's just equal parts of Herbsaint liqueur and Angostura bitters. Obviously you don't need to mix up more than an ounce or two at a time.

INTRODUCTION

Welcome to *Outlander* Cocktails!

*Diana Gabaldon's series of books, and the TV series based on them,
have won over millions of fans who have developed a thirst for her particular blend of
historical time travel, romance, war, intrigue, family loyalty, passion, and a bit
of magic. This book aims at satisfying that thirst, at least in liquid form, by presenting a
cornucopia of drink recipes and food accompaniments that touch upon these themes.
As such, they are centered on but not exclusively bound to the geographic locations
and historical periods encompassed by* Outlander.

What were they drinking back in mid-eighteenth-century Scotland? Or on the Caribbean Islands? Or in the Carolina colonies a few decades later? "Whisky!" comes the immediate reply. And rum, wine, ale, and cider, and that's about it. The trouble with sticking to absolutely authentic period recipes is that none of those categories of liquid tasted the same as those made today, and the range of available ingredients to mix with was far more limited. If all the recipes here were based solely on historical ingredients and recipes, this would be a much shorter book. Even the Europe and the United States of the 1960s and 1970s, though wonderfully evoked in the books and shows with a heaping helping of nostalgia, were not a rich period of cocktail creations—modern bartenders often refer to this time as a Dark Ages of drinking, when vodka eclipsed aged spirits, and convenient industrial products like sour mix replaced fresh juices. By comparison, the present day is a veritable cocktail renaissance of classic recipes and bold new experimentation. Freshly sourced and high-quality mixing ingredients are more widely available than ever; the distillery industry is booming worldwide; and the craft movement has produced, and continues to produce, a fantastic range of artisanal spirits, wines, beers, ciders, and other mixological delights.

Tastes have changed since the eighteenth century, and we should generally be thankful for that! We no longer have a taste for meat that's been hung up until it's far beyond "well-aged," we are much less likely to boil all our vegetables to death, and that "braw dram" back then would not necessarily appeal to modern palates. One theme of *Outlander* that actually has come back into vogue is herbal medicine, and while modern medicine has debunked the idea of alcohol as "good for ye," many of the recipes do rely on herbal ingredients, and there are low- and no-alcohol offerings as well.

But perhaps the best reason for moving beyond history is the source itself. One of the most abiding impressions *Outlander* gives us is the sheer joy of life and the willingness to partake of its pleasures—to grow and change, even amid the violence and sorrows that Claire, Jamie, Bree, Roger, and all the other characters endure. If they were to step into our homes today, they would surely delight in the full range of drinks now available. And so should we.

All this explanation may be enough to make you reach for the whisky bottle already and be done with it. But this book is intended to do more than simply meet the demand for a drink. It aims to engage those completely new to mixing cocktails as well as seasoned home bartenders. As such, the recipes here are written to encourage you to go beyond what's familiar, to experiment with new flavors, to develop your own palates, to embrace your passion all in the spirit (so to speak!) of *Outlander*.

So, a few ground rules before we begin may be helpful.

1. TASTE WIDELY. Whether you are already familiar with different styles and expressions of spirits, be willing to try lots of drinks and ingredients. Try what's new, what's local, even what you don't think you'll like. The worst that can happen is that you'll confirm something you don't like, but just as easily you may find a new favorite or even discover that something you swore was absolutely not your thing is actually . . . pretty damn tasty. Along the way you'll realize that taste is subjective: we don't always taste even the same thing the same way because our mood, the environment, or the circumstances are different. You'll start to build your own narrative of tastes.

2. TRUST YOUR OWN TASTE. The internet abounds with top ten lists and expert panelists and influencers all telling us what we should like. And their advice can be helpful, particularly when they dispense valuable information: tasting notes, what makes different expressions of the same spirit taste differently, or what's new and exciting. But since taste is subjective, and it's your drink, you should be comfortable deciding what you like and not feel pressured to like something just because some expert says it's the best or it's what everyone else is drinking. It all comes down to finding what tastes good in your own glass.

3. REMEMBER THAT COCKTAILS ARE ABOUT MORE THAN JUST THE TASTE. Anyone who's watched an expert bartender prepare and serve a drink knows that it's a feast for all the senses: the play of light on cut crystal and metal, the immediate Pavlovian response to the swirl of ice in the mixing glass, the color of the cocktail and its garnish, and the aroma as you lift it to your lips . . . all these come before the actual taste and shape how we experience it. Therefore, don't neglect the details that go toward enhancing this experience—glassware, garnishes, ice, and more (see page 36).

4. CREATE YOUR OWN STORIES. You don't need to read Proust to know that our senses of taste and smell are closely connected with memory. The recipes in this book act not only as connections to your memories of the series but also as springboards to creating new memories. Every cocktail has a story to it, starting with who created it, where, and when; but that story continues with everyone who makes it and what goes on while you're drinking it, and it becomes a story you return to every time you mix an old favorite. So share these drinks with friends, family, lovers, and more; tell your stories about how you first tried this or that drink, or the night that an experiment went wrong, or the crazy thing that someone said when they first tasted . . . you get the idea. It's your story; live it!

HISTORICAL NOTES
on Whisky *and* Other Spirits

Some background on the state of the distiller's art, both during the eighteenth century and today, will help position the drink recipes in the historical context of the books and within current cocktail trends. Here you'll learn more about how modern distilled spirits evolved, how they're being used in cocktails these days, and how spirits producers are constantly balancing commitment to tradition and culture with pursuing innovation and new marketing opportunities. If you just want to get to the recipes, feel free to skip this section, but who knows? You might learn something new!

SCOTCH WHISKY

Scotch whisky, one of the world's most iconic and storied distilled spirits, is intimately bound to Scottish history and culture. Many books have been written about its origin, evolution, culture, and economics, and of course its myriad expressions, so these notes will be confined to a brief history covering the periods in which *Outlander* is set and some discussion on the use of Scotch whisky in cocktails.

Whisky in mid-eighteenth-century Scotland was mostly a "craft" operation by necessity: farmers and local still owners would malt barley, dry it over a fire, ferment it, and distill it in small pot stills. This would produce a rather rough spirit, as Claire could attest to from her first sip of the 1740s vintage just a few hours after traveling through the standing stones. This kind of whisky would typically be consumed fairly quickly: wooden casks were for storing and transporting the stuff; long aging was the exception rather than

the rule. In this sense it was almost all "single malt," technically, a spirit made of 100 percent malted barley distilled in one place, by a particular still, during one distilling season. While today we think of single malts as the pinnacle of the craft, it's a relatively recent phenomenon: marketing single malts from individual distilleries as a superior spirit to blended Scotch was an idea that only took off outside of Scotland in the 1990s.

In the Lowlands, closer to the border, there were the beginnings of a more industrial approach, where whisky merchants contracted with local farmers for larger amounts of malted barley and other grains that would be distilled and shipped south to England for the Sassenachs to drink. These producers would have spent more time and expertise blending whisky from multiple distillers to achieve a balanced and consistent taste, but ironically, the average Scot would never have tasted it unless they visited England. And by the 1740s, some share of Scottish distillers' product, particularly the cheapest kind made from multiple varieties of low-quality grains, was even being flavored and used to satisfy the growing English demand for gin. It's quite possible that Scottish know-how was employed here as well. Scotch whisky expert Andrew Derbidge explains:

> To make it more palatable, the spirit (new made Scotch) was often supplemented with numerous flavorings and additives such as herbs, spices, and other botanical infusions. As late as 1755, nine years after the Battle of Culloden, there is a reference to whisky being defined as a "compounded distilled spirit, being drawn on aromatics." The movements and activities of Bonnie Prince Charlie after the Battle of Culloden are only hinted at in the Outlander series, but it is known he escaped to the west coast of Scotland and spent a few weeks on the Isle of Skye before eventually finding passage back to France. A well-known whisky liqueur, Drambuie (a blend of whisky infused with honey, herbs, and spices), claims its origins can be traced to a secret recipe created for the prince by his physician. According to legend, Bonnie Prince Charlie gave the elixir and its recipe to a Scottish clan on Skye as a gesture of thanks for their hospitality and protection. Possibly rooted more in opportunistic marketing rather than fact, it's a good brand-origin story, but it certainly demonstrates that whisky was being mixed with other ingredients to create new drinks.

When Claire and Frank took their fateful trip to Inverness in 1947, the whisky industry was just starting to recover from a wartime cessation of distilling and postwar shortages. For most of the twentieth century, blended Scotch still dominated sales; single malts like the Glenfiddich they shared after seeing the "ghost" were almost unknown outside of Scotland at this time.

Using Scotch in Cocktails

Scotch whisky is largely underrepresented when it comes to contemporary cocktails. There are a handful of "classics" from the earlier twentieth century, such as the Rob Roy, the Blood and Sand, and the Bobby Burns—many of which are simply variants of other classics like the Manhattan—with Scotch subbing for bourbon or rye. It's true that, compared to those other whiskies, Scotch can be trickier to work with; its flavor notes don't always harmonize well with traditional mixers. Another reason for its lack of use may be a persistent, misconceived notion that Scotch is only supposed to be sipped on its own, perhaps with a few drops of water, or at most a single ice cube. But there is way more to Scotch than peat bombs or sherry-aged elixirs worth a laird's ransom. And if smoky flavor equals an unappealing cocktail to some, then why the current rage for mezcal drinks, which prominently highlight similar smoky notes? Some of the most famous new classic cocktails, such as the Penicillin, are made with Scotch! Slowly, bartenders and enthusiasts in the twenty-first century are overcoming their prejudice against using good Scotch in cocktails, and the whisky industry is taking notice. A number of distillers are marketing younger, often unpeated single malts as entry points to the world of Scotch, and they are both inexpensive and tasty enough to use in cocktails. Other distillers are experimenting with different types of barley and nontraditional methods of barrel aging and finishing, resulting in whiskies with unusual flavor notes that open up new possibilities.

If this book can help dispel the myth of Scotch whisky's unsuitability for cocktails, then it will have served a noble purpose, one perhaps worthy of the heroic protagonists of *Outlander.* To finish with another quote from Mr. Derbidge: "From the floral, grassy whiskies of the Lowlands, to the sweet, fruity, and sherried whiskies of Speyside, right up to the robust, peaty, and smoky malts of Islay, there's a Scotch whisky–based cocktail for every nuance, mood, style, and occasion. And that's something worth travelling through time for!"

AMERICAN WHISKEY

You caught the spelling change, right? There's no good reason other than tradition for the additional "e," which is accepted in the United States and Ireland but is left out in Scotland, Japan, and Canada. The most famous styles of American whiskey are bourbon and rye, and they are the ones most frequently employed in this book. Of the two, rye may be the older, given that rye is an Old World grain that was carried to the Americas by colonists, and found a suitable climate for growing in the northern colonies. Bourbon, which by law must contain 51 percent or more of corn, began to be produced in the warmer climate of the southern colonies, where corn was the more common crop. Whatever the grain, the fertility of American soils provided abundant resources for distillers, and colonial accounts attest to the prodigious quantities of alcohol made and consumed by European colonists, or traded to Native Americans, despite Claire's protest in *Drums of Autumn*. American whiskey during this period was much like Jamie's product: young, rough, and raw. Similarly to Scotch production, the industry grew, matured, and made significant improvements during the nineteenth and early twentieth centuries. Unlike Scotch, however, American whiskey took a big hit during Prohibition and as late as the 1990s languished far behind other spirits, even in the United States. The current American whiskey revival was powered by multiple factors. First, the rise of single malt Scotches, along with their rise in price, led drinkers to search for less expensive whiskies but also to see high-end bourbons and ryes in a manner similar to single malts—as unique expressions of *terroire* and the distiller's craft. Second, the cocktail renaissance around the turn of the twenty-first century repopularized many classic American whiskey cocktails. Third, craft distillers brought back the use of local grains and employed both old historical and new nontraditional production and aging methods. Lastly, the rise of the internet fueled speculation on all manner of distilled spirits and virtually created the current fad for rare, limited release, and unusual styles. Many bartenders reach for a higher-proof whiskey, either bottled in bond (100 proof) or cask strength (usually 104 proof or higher) when making cocktails, because the greater potency will help the flavor come through when mixed with other ingredients.

Using American Whiskey in Cocktails

BOURBON: The sweetness of corn together with bourbon's mandatory aging in charred oak barrels create the dominant notes of caramel and vanilla, along with grain, fruity, floral, spicy, and many other flavors. Bourbon has a natural affinity for other sweet ingredients and is usually paired with lemon, although tropical-style bourbon drinks with lime do exist and work quite well. Cinnamon and other baking spices are also excellent partners. Similar to Scotch, some higher-end bourbons are now being finished in port, sherry, rum, and wine barrels, imparting different flavors and expanding the mixing possibilities.

RYE: Differences in the taste of the grain itself, along with differences in the distillation process, produce a spirit that is noticeably spicier than the average bourbon, with taste notes that can include not just rye bread but black pepper, clove, and even mint and dill! Rye powered many classic, pre-Prohibition cocktails, but its revival took longer than bourbon's, and production of rye still lags far behind. Craft distillers are testing heirloom varieties of rye and attempting to re-create historic regional styles of rye whiskey, even to the point of reviving antiquated still technologies in search of long-lost flavors.

Rye is nice with anything spicy, particularly baking spices, and is a winner with bitter liqueurs and amari. It pairs perfectly with vermouth and works well with lemon, orange, and pineapple; adventurous bartenders are even using it in tropical-style drinks. As distillers continue to expand the range of rye whiskey expressions, its cocktail potential will continue to broaden.

Other American Whiskeys

The American whiskey revival truly arrived when some distillers recently started developing the idea of American single malt—barley-based whiskey to rival Scotch itself—and some of their current expressions stand up very well. But not all American whiskey is sticking to traditional styles. Large and small producers alike are going hog wild on experimentation: including unusual grains such as buckwheat, rice, or sorghum; smoking their grains with Texas oak, mesquite, or other woods; finishing whiskey in everything from apricot brandy to maple syrup to vermouth casks. The sheer diversity of methods and expressions goes beyond the wildest dreams of the distillers of yore and will likely continue to increase as producers seek out new flavors and new ways to create something unique. It's a great time to be an American whiskey drinker.

RUM

Compared to Scotch whisky, rum is a much more diverse spirit and is more difficult to define or categorize. Its historical development is also inextricably bound with the horrors of the African slave trade, which Claire and Jamie come to experience personally in *Voyager, Drums of Autumn,* and *The Fiery Cross.* During the eighteenth century, the Caribbean was the center of global rum production. In British colonies such as Jamaica, each sugarcane plantation typically had its own still to convert the skimmings (the froth and debris that floated to the top of the cane syrup as it was boiled down) and molasses left over from sugar production into a valuable, exportable commodity. Records of the time show Jamaican rum fetching prices in England equal to or exceeding the cost of brandy from the Continent. French and Spanish colonies were discouraged from producing rum, but much of their molasses was shipped to New England, serving as the raw material for one leg of the infamous triangle trade. No matter where it was distilled, the methods were essentially the same; there were no distinct "styles" of rum, and just like the bulk of Scotch whisky of the same time, very little of it was aged beyond the time it took to move it from its place of origin to where it was sold and consumed. As the century progressed and the rum industry expanded on the backs of enslaved African labor, London became a global leader of the rum trade to the point where a whole series of warehouses known as Rum Quay were built adjacent to the West India docks on the Thames, the better to house the thousands of barrels that were aged, blended, and transported throughout the empire.

The nineteenth and early twentieth centuries saw the same advances in distillation technology that overtook the whisky industry and the development of regional styles of rum based on their cultural heritage: British, French, or Spanish. In the postwar years, many producers went light, trying to compete with vodka and gin. Only recently has the trend turned back toward long-aged, rich, and complex rums, some of which now command the same level of cachet (and corresponding high prices) of high-end whiskies and brandies.

Using Rum in Cocktails

If the primary myth of Scotch is that it's not supposed to be used for cocktails, the primary myth of rum may be that you can tell what it tastes like based on the color. Clear rum indicates a young spirit, light and clean in flavor; and the darker you go, the older and richer it must be. This just isn't true. Different rums (English), or *rhums* (French), or *rones* (Spanish), depending on the language spoken, produce an extraordinary diversity of flavors, depending on the raw material used (fresh-pressed sugarcane juice or molasses), the distillation process (pot-still, single column, or multicolumn), the length and climate and type of barrels it's aged in, and perhaps most surprisingly, what's done before bottling. You

About Spiced Rum

Spiced rum is usually made from young molasses-based rums with added flavorings, typically cinnamon, nutmeg, and allspice, and caramel coloring. It capitalizes on a long tradition of infusing a bottle of rum with spices, herbs, and other flavors in the home. While many serious mixologists stay far away from spiced rum and its industrial flavorings, you could try a spiced rum in any drink that uses an aged rum if you want to add those baking spice notes to a drink without any hassle. However, if you're willing to sweat the details and use bitters and/or the infusions, tinctures, and simple syrup recipes included here, you will end up with a better-tasting drink. Ultimately, it's your call.

may or may not know that clear-colored rums can in fact be aged and strong flavored—they're just filtered to remove color. So-called "dark" rums are not necessarily any older than their clear counterparts, and they are often colored with caramel and have other ingredients to add flavor and mimic the appearance of older rum. Such additives are not always disclosed on the label or in the brand's marketing. It gets no better when it comes to age statements. Whereas whisky generally adheres to international standards that require that, for example, a bottle labeled "12-year-old whisky" will be 100 percent whisky aged at least 12 years, rum-producing countries have as yet no comprehensive standards. This means a rum labeled "12-year-old" may be all 12-year-aged spirit, or multiple spirits with an average age of 12 years, or rum, some amount of which is aged 12 years. Without getting an advanced degree in rumology, the best way to know what you're drinking is to read the labels carefully and have some understanding of different styles.

Light rums work best paired with bright, clean flavors like citrus and other tropical fruits or with baking spices like ginger and cinnamon. Good-quality aged rums can often be subbed for whisky in many classic cocktails but also bring a broad range of flavors

that play well with bitter liqueurs, amari, sherries, and more. Dark rums are typically paired with fruit juices in high-octane cocktails, but a small amount can also be added or "floated" on top of a drink for a hit of molasses scent and flavor. Rhum Agricole, Clairin, and other rhums distilled from wild, fermented, fresh-pressed cane juice are a whole different category; they usually exhibit fresh grassy, vegetal, or even oily flavors and must be used in a cocktail that specifically calls for them.

BRANDY

Aged grape brandy is quite probably the most glorious French contribution to mixology, though Gallic entries into the liqueur category are by no means a distant second. Brandy in the mid-eighteenth century had neither appellation d'origine designations nor celebrity endorsements, but in contrast to the nascent Scotch whisky industry, high-quality long-aged brandies had already achieved a reputation and a market that reached far beyond the renowned Cognac and Armagnac regions.

Brandy is often assumed to have been the drink of the rich due to the cost of aging—and in the case of British Isles imbibers, the cost of importing the stuff (legally or otherwise) from the Continent. But just like their counterparts in Scotland, French farmers

Apple Brandy

Although not produced in the same volume as grape brandies, calvados and other apple brandies share a very similar long history. Speaking of which, the oldest distiller in the United States, Laird & Company, was founded by a Scottish family in the early 1700s and is still well known for the quality of their apple brandy. Straight apple brandy, French or otherwise, can be substituted in recipes calling for grape brandy, but bartenders these days are also using it as an ingredient in its own right, and a number of craft producers in the United States are entering the market. Apple brandy is used similarly to grape brandy in cocktails, but its lighter, softer flavors allow it to be widely paired with other spirits or just mixed with soda or tonic water as a refreshing apéritif. However, do not mistake blended applejack or apple-flavored brandy for the real deal, 100 percent straight apple brandy; the former are inexpensive grain distillates flavored with small amounts of apple brandy and/or industrial flavorings.

and local landowners harvested their own grapes (and apples, pears, and almost any kind of fruit that was on hand) and distilled their own brandies and eaux-de-vie for local consumption. And as for other uses, while brandy-based liqueurs like Bénédictine and Chartreuse may not have histories as long as their advertising may suggest, the use of brandy as a vehicle for medicines, often including dozens of herbal ingredients, is as old as distilling technology itself.

Most brandy, with the partial exception of Armagnac, is blended from multiple sources and age ranges. For cocktails, a younger expression, often labeled VS or with no age statement, will work perfectly fine: the predominantly fruity, floral taste notes pair well with any number of ingredients. Several producers are now marketing French and American brandies that are blended specifically for use in cocktails. An older brandy, labeled VSOP or XO, with its richer flavor and stronger wood influence, is best reserved for a special cocktail with minimal mixers, to let the brandy shine through. These days, many countries produce grape brandies. Some expressions are world-class; others are mass-produced, inexpensive products that may work fine in cocktails but won't have the same complex flavor. It's best to sample one before subbing it in a recipe that calls for brandy.

GIN

Taste a bottle of modern gin and a bottle of modern Scotch, and you'd never guess that they stem from a common origin. We've already learned about Scottish distillate being sold to make gin in the early eighteenth century; if that seems odd, it becomes less so if you know that *genever*, the precursor to modern gin, was essentially a flavored whisky. Low Country distillers used a mash of malted barley as their base, just like the Scottish, but then tamed and flavored the resulting spirit with juniper berries and sometimes other herbs and spices that were believed to have medicinal properties. In fact, given how frequently the Scots were adding botanicals to their whisky, the dividing line between early whisky and genever is so slim as to be nearly nonexistent. A thirst for genever accompanied the coronation of William of Orange as king of England in 1689, as it was the national drink of his birthplace. Although German Hanoverians sat on the English throne during *Outlander*'s eighteenth-century settings, gin reigned supreme as the infamous drink of the poor and working classes of England until the Gin Acts and a series of bad grain harvests caused its downfall in the mid-1700s. Genever and gin also quickly crossed the Atlantic to the British colonies and, according to genever expert Philip Duff, had a strong influence on the establishment of early American whiskey distilling. During the nineteenth century, gin gradually rehabilitated its image as a more refined spirit suitable for the wealthier classes. Up until fairly late in the century, gin was usually sweetened and took on some color and flavor from the wood barrels it was stored in. The most popular modern style of gin, London dry, only developed in the last decades of the 1800s through more refined distilling technology and a shift in the public's taste toward a less sweet gin that emphasized the botanical ingredients. Alas, by the time Brianna and Roger met and fell in love in the late 1960s, gin had fallen once more, this time to vodka and light rum, which were seen as more modern and stylish. The rise of the modern cocktail movement proved the death of gin was prematurely announced and has fueled a boom in brands and styles.

Using Gin and Genever in Cocktails

Genever is little known outside of the Low Countries, and that's a shortfall that this book seeks to rectify. Even aside from the historical roots, it's a full-flavored, versatile spirit, and some high-quality brands are now exported to the States. Blended genever is lighter in color and flavor and perhaps more ginlike in its ability to mix with many different flavors. Single malt genever is its own thing—you have to taste it to really understand it, and it works well with stronger partners, similar to other styles of whisky. As for gin, there are multiple styles of modern gin, and the category is rapidly becoming more diverse. While London dry gin is the Greenwich meridian of modern gin and the base for almost all classic gin cocktails, it is by no means the only style around these days. Old Tom gins are contemporary re-creations of the historical eighteenth-century style of gin. They are usually but not always sweetened and are often aged in wood. Contrary to what was just said about rum, color does give a reliable indicator of taste for Old Tom: pale or straw-colored gins are lighter and closer to London dry; darker color results from more time in wooden barrels, which gives them additional flavor and a more whisky-like character. Regardless of length of aging, Old Tom gins are not interchangeable with London dry gins.

New Western was a term coined in the early 2000s by American distiller Ryan Magarian to describe new craft gins that downplayed the juniper and upped other flavors. Similarly, nontraditional gins have taken this cue and run all over the globe with it. Top-ranked gins from India, Japan, South Africa, Spain, and elsewhere often include indigenous or locally popular ingredients and have truly broadened the possibilities for gin as a category of spirits. These newer styles will often work in recipes calling for London dry, but they will taste different. It will require a bit of experimentation for you to find out what works with what, and adjustments to a recipe may be necessary—but that's part of the fun.

A Warning about Alcohol

Anyone who has a passing acquaintance with Claire's medical practices in the eighteenth century is aware of her frustrations with the misguided understandings and habits of her patients. While it may be obvious to say that things have improved since then, there is still a surprising amount of misinformation and dubious claims being made in the media about alcohol and health. Simply put, no amount of alcohol is "healthy," and overconsumption will inevitably lead to serious health risks. We encourage readers to drink responsibly.

MAKING *the* DRINKS
in This Book

Here are recommendations for setting up your home bar. In some cases, particular brands are recommended; in others, any example of a category of spirit will work. For spirits and liqueurs that are unfamiliar to you, it's a smart idea to try them before buying an entire bottle, and keep in mind the amounts used in recipes when deciding whether to buy a full-size bottle or a smaller one, if available.

STOCKING YOUR HOME BAR

SCOTCH: In order to make the Scotch drinks in this book, you will need at least a few different bottles. The first and most important is a bottle of blended malt Scotch, such as Monkey Shoulder. Second, a bottle of peated single malt, such as Laphroaig or another Islay single malt. And last, a bottle of unpeated, sherry-aged single malt. These should not be the most expensive brands, nor do they need to be, but quality does tell in cocktails. Try tasting different brands, whether a blended malt, made entirely of single malt stocks, or a less expensive blended Scotch that includes grain whisky, and see what a difference it makes to your drinks.

BOURBON: High-end, limited-release bourbons now command astronomical prices, but you'll be glad to know that perfectly good cocktail bourbons don't have to be expensive or extra aged. And while Kentucky produces the largest amount of bourbon in the United States by far, it does not legally have to come from the Bluegrass State. Start with a bottled in bond bourbon; the higher proof stands up better in cocktails. Try a small-batch or single-barrel bourbon if you want to up your cocktail game, but keep in mind that the taste profile changes somewhat from year to year and barrel to barrel. More expensive bourbons finished in sherry, wine, or port barrels are now common and, just like finished Scotch whisky, can impart extra flavors into a cocktail. Always be willing to check out local craft bourbons. You may find a new favorite and support a small business at the same time.

RYE: It's basically an open secret that the most frequently used ryes in high-end cocktail establishments are inexpensive brands like Rittenhouse and Old Overholt. Why? Because they are high quality for the price and work really well in cocktails. At this point, rye whiskey is still a much smaller category than bourbon with fewer expressions available, though its popularity and diversity are rising. Mainstream American ryes often have a significant amount of corn in the mash bill, creating sweet bourbonlike flavors. A number of craft distillers and Canadian rye producers use a much higher percentage of rye, which gives a spicier, drier profile. Just as with bourbon, single-barrel ryes offer higher proof and more distinctive flavor profiles, and various barrel finishes—from apricot brandy to rum—are now appearing. Start with a benchmark brand like those mentioned above, but then try "high rye" and higher-end expressions from outfits like Dad's Hat, High West, Lot 40, Russell's Reserve, Sagamore Spirit, WhistlePig, and many more.

RUM: Many of the rum recipes in this book, especially those leaning historically, should be made with a good-quality, aged, pot-still rum. Several brands from Jamaica (Appleton Estate, Smith & Cross), Barbados (Mount Gay, Plantation, The Real McCoy), and Guyana (El Dorado, Lemon Hart) produce fine examples of this style, which lean toward funky, ripe fruit flavors in the Jamaican and darker, smokier notes in the Guyanese. Other recipes may employ light rum, meaning a lightly aged "white" or light-colored blended molasses-based rum, typified by examples from former Spanish colonies (Flor de Caña, Ron Diplomático Blanco, Don Q), although many countries produce very good light rum these days (Plantation 3 Stars, El Dorado 3 Year, Banks 5 Island, Denizen). Aged agricole rhums (Rhum J.M., Rhum Clement, Neisson) can often be employed in drinks that call for Cognac and offer an equal level of taste and complexity. Any drinks made with other rum styles will be specified in the recipe notes: be careful not to substitute rums without knowing the differences!

GIN: As blended Scotch is to the whisky drinks in this book, London dry is to the gin drinks: it's the benchmark cocktail standard. While there are expressions ranging from cheap to very expensive, you're most likely to find your sweet spot somewhere in the middle (Beefeater, Fords, Tanqueray, Sipsmith). That being said, there are now high-end gins worth splurging for that are masterpieces of botanical complexity (Monkey 47, KI NO BI, Nolet's). Cocktails calling for Old Tom gin require just that; it's a very different beast from London dry (Ransom Old Tom, Barr Hill Tomcat, Hayman's). You may try substituting New Western (Aviation, NYDC Dorothy Parker, Bluecoat) or other nontraditional gins (The Botanist, Four Pillars, St. George Terroir, Gin Mare, and many others) for London dry, but as mentioned above, the flavor will be different and may not work in all recipes. But don't let that stop you from trying; there are many high-quality, unique gin expressions out these days, from local craft distillers to international offerings!

VERMOUTH: From the medieval German *vermut* meaning wormwood, but perfected in the Italian peninsula in the early nineteenth century, vermouth is a style of fortified wine with wormwood and other botanicals macerated in it. The most popular styles are sweet vermouth, essential for Manhattans and Negronis, and dry vermouth, aka the Martini's other ingredient. But don't stop with that; *bianco* vermouths are coming back into fashion—lighter and more floral than red and sweeter than dry, with a wide variety of tasting notes. Some producers are experimenting with other in-between styles called *ambre* (amber) or *rubino* (ruby), and other nontraditional expressions have been created by American, Spanish, and even Japanese companies. Make sure to store opened bottles in the refrigerator, just like wine, to preserve their flavor.

SHERRY: It's downright tragic that sherry still suffers from an unfair label as a boring, unfashionable, stuck-in-the-past style of wine. Despite being the best kept secret in cocktails for decades, most whisky drinkers know sherry only as the stuff that flavors the

barrels that whisky is aged in—Spain now exports more sherry barrels used for finishing other spirits than it exports bottles of sherry! Knowing a bit about sherry styles will help you identify the flavor notes it adds to cocktails as well as sherry-finished Scotch. Fino is the youngest and driest expression of this fortified wine and can be used just like dry vermouth; it adds notes of almonds and a savory, doughy flavor to drinks. Amontillado, the sherry most commonly used in cocktails, is quite variable but balances acidity and dry fruit flavors with more savory spice and nutty notes and is used similarly to sweet vermouth or lighter amari. Oloroso is rich and complex, with a nutty bouquet, and has wood, leather, and balsamic flavor notes. It is usually mixed with richly flavored aged whiskies and rums. Cream, Moscatel, and Pedro Ximénez styles are sweet and raisiny: add them in small amounts to rich, dessert-style cocktails.

AMARI: It's no exaggeration that one reason for the current cocktail renaissance has been a seismic shift in popular taste toward the bitter. Bitter foods like kale and arugula, dark chocolate, and artisanal vinegars that became all the rage in the 1980s and early 1990s accustomed palates to the delights of amari—a class of bitter liqueurs from Italy, France, and now many other countries including the United States. Often employed in new classic drinks in smaller amounts to offset the sweetness of vermouths, fruit juices, and simple syrups, amari are also becoming favored when paired with spirits like whisky or mezcal in equal-portion shots or short cocktails. There are many styles of amari, and whole books have been written about them, but here are a few to get acquainted with.

- CLASSIC APERITIVO AMARI are generally lighter in flavor and often include bitter citrus and/or baking spices to perk up the appetite. Look for Aperol, Amaro Nonino, Cardamaro, and Meletti.

- DIGESTIVO AMARI are darker and stronger in flavor; they're a natural pairing with aged distilled spirits. Try Averna, Amaro Lucano, St. Agrestis Amaro, and many more.

- ALPINE-STYLE AMARI balance the bitterness with flavors of menthol, pine, and spice. Look for Braulio, Faccia Brutto Centerbe, and Varnelli Amaro Sibilla.

- FERNETS, which are considered a separate category from amari by some authorities, are usually powerfully bitter with strong—some might say overwhelming—flavors of licorice, mint, and woody, leathery spice notes. There's Fernet Branca, Branca Menta, Fernet del Frate, and Fernet Vallet, among others. American and Mexican distillers as well as other Italian brands also produce fernets, some of which are less ferocious. Try them if you find Fernet Branca overpowering.

As with many other types of spirits, new, nontraditional expressions are pushing the boundaries of amari and incorporating all manner of ingredients from cacao and dandelion root to tea and tangerine, and even arugula!

COCKTAIL EQUIPMENT and TECHNIQUES

There are many excellent cocktail books out there giving solid advice on tools and basic techniques and abundant online how-to videos on stirring, shaking, and more. Rather than reinventing the wheel, this section gives you recommendations on useful bar tools and how to use them, along with some remarks on a much less often discussed topic: why drinks are made a particular way.

You can create excellent cocktails with nothing more than a glass, a spoon, and something to measure liquids. There are at least two reasons bartenders have more equipment. First, proper tools simply make the job easier. A barspoon is long and straight to enable good stirring technique. A jigger makes measuring and pouring ingredients faster and more reliable than eyeballing with a kitchen measuring cup. A Hawthorne strainer fits perfectly over a mixing glass or tin to keep the drink free of ice shards, citrus seeds, and muddled ingredients. The second reason has to do with the notion that a good cocktail should engage all the senses, and mixing a drink is not just a process but a performance. Polished metal and cut crystal catch the light and add to the visual appeal. Weighted, balanced shaker tins allow for confident, controlled shaking and create that unmistakable ice-on-tin sound that gets the taste buds salivating. When called for, a spritz of bitters or a flamed garnish releases a perfumed cloud that envelops the drink. All these enhance the drinking experience. So, before you invest in boxes of fancy tools and a closet full of glassware, ask yourself: Will this help me make drinks more easily? Will it add to the overall experience of drinking? Will it make things more fun?

ESSENTIAL TOOLS

- JIGGER. The essential measuring instrument, most useful in the sizes of 1 to 2 ounces, and ½ to ¾ ounce. Metal is generally preferred for ease of cleaning.

- MIXING GLASS. A good mixing glass is wider and heavier than a standard pint glass, which makes it more stable. Clear glass allows you to see what's going on inside as you measure and stir.

- SHAKER. Whether you prefer the cobbler shaker that comes with its own strainer built in or the Boston two-piece shaker, either will work much better than any improvised kit.

- HAWTHORNE STRAINER. Essential for stirred drinks, it is less essential if you use a cobbler shaker.

- Y-SHAPED VEGETABLE PEELER. Makes cutting citrus garnishes much easier and safer than using a knife.

Additional Tools

- CITRUS PRESS. Always freshly squeeze your citrus juices. This tool makes juicing simple unless you already have an electric juice extractor on hand!

- MUDDLER. For pressing herbs, mashing fruits, and crushing sugar cubes in the mixing glass. Avoid muddlers with teeth or wooden ones that are varnished: the former get bits of stuff stuck in them, and you don't need varnish in your drink.

- METAL STRAWS. More sustainable but also carry the cold of the drink to your lips, which is particularly refreshing in hot weather. A worthy upgrade for tall drinks or those with crushed ice.

- FINE GRATER. Some drinks call for citrus zest or grated spices. Particularly for spices like nutmeg, freshly grated is essential.

GLASSWARE

Of all the styles and sizes of glasses that you may encounter in a bar or restaurant, a few qualify as essential, or at least highly useful, for the drinks in this book. Put your glasses in the freezer for at least 15 minutes before serving, or fill them with ice to chill before you start mixing, then dump the ice before adding the drink.

- COUPE. The classic shape of a coupe glass holds most standard cocktails with little room to spare. The stem keeps your hand and fingers isolated from the drink, which keeps the liquid colder for longer. And the wide rim gives space for garnishes or flavored rims. Also called a cocktail glass.

- OLD-FASHIONED OR ROCKS GLASS. The squat shape and thick walls give this glass heft that's appropriate for strong, spirit-forward drinks. It's large enough to hold a single large ice cube or a handful if called for, but not so large that the drink appears meager inside.

- COLLINS GLASS. Tall and thin, it's built to hold a lot of ice, and the narrow diameter holds in bubbles for drinks with carbonated components. It practically begs for a straw sticking out of the top, preferably adjacent to a fresh, colorful garnish.

- NICK AND NORA GLASS. Perhaps not essential, but an elegant choice for stirred drinks, especially spirit-forward styles served up with no ice. The smaller size is a useful reminder to consume in moderation.

RE-USING CITRUS/FRUITS

Using all parts of your ingredients is a notion common to colonial householding as well as modern sustainability. Bars and restaurants also minimize waste to keep costs down. Some of these techniques work best in commercial kitchens, but here are two ideas, one historical and one modern, to stretch your budget as well as extend flavor. *Oleo saccharum,* Latin for "oil sugar," is an essential step for making the quintessential drink of the seventeenth century: punch. To make it, wash and dry your citrus, and then, before juicing it, peel the fruit, trying to avoid the white pith underneath the skin. Place the peels in a glass jar with a lid, add enough sugar to cover, put the lid on, and shake vigorously. Let it sit for an hour or so and the sugar will draw the oils out of the skin to create your oleo saccharum. Mix it with fresh juice to up the flavor, or substitute it for simple syrup. Citrus stock is a similar idea created by the Trash Tiki cocktail pop-up team members, using the whole fruit after juicing. Unless you've just juiced a dozen or more fruits, it's easier to keep spent citrus shells in the freezer until you've accumulated several cups. Then bring the same number of cups of water to a boil, add the citrus shells, and simmer for 5 minutes. Remove the citrus and let cool. Measure the stock, put it back on the heat, and simmer until it's been reduced by half. Add a scant ¼ cup of sugar for each cup of stock, and then adjust the acidity to your liking by adding a teaspoon or more of fresh lemon and/or fresh-pressed tart apple juice.

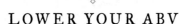

LOWER YOUR ABV

Many classic cocktail recipes are heavy on distilled spirits, relying on vermouth or other mixers as supporting actors. Flipping the script can result in a drink that's lighter in alcohol by volume (ABV) but no less flavorful; consider a reverse Manhattan or Martini, and then apply the same trick to some of the spirit-forward recipes here and see how it goes! This is not a universal rule, though; it won't work as well when the other ingredients are only fruit juices or very sweet liqueurs or syrups. Also consider ditching the distilled spirits entirely and trying drinks based entirely on vermouth or sherry; you'll get a lot of flavor without as much alcohol.

SPLIT BASES

Some spirits have close friends. When put together, they each contribute some of their own personality, forming an agreeable union. Whisky and aged rum can make great partners as long as you think through matching the flavor notes a bit. Rye and Cognac are a dynamic duo that go way back to the birth of the cocktail in the nineteenth century. Gin and brandy may seem surprising, but they appear in a couple of classic cocktails and can be employed elsewhere, especially if the gin is a barrel-aged one. Mezcal and tequila are a natural pair the same way peated and unpeated Scotches are used in modern classic cocktails, and mezcal is now also being paired with rye and bourbon to similar effect. Apple brandy of good quality can hang with almost anything, contributing sweet fruit flavors and rounding out the hard corners of other spirits. Try a split-base cocktail and you may find one of these combos to be frequent visitors in your drinks.

ONE

Apéritifs

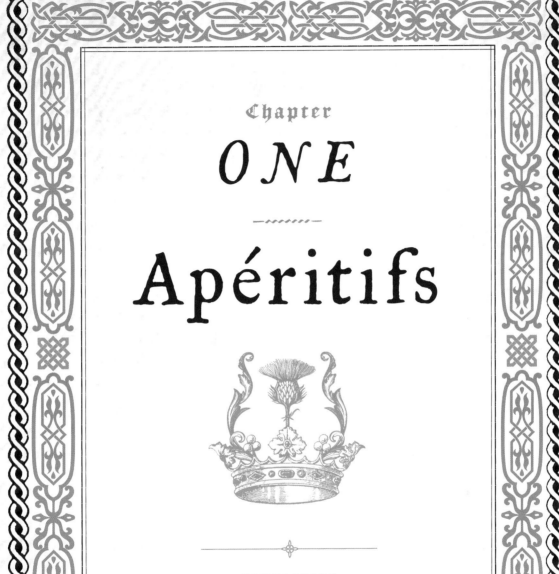

CONTAINING

Six Recipes

Brandy-and-Splash, Bittersweet

IF WE START AT the very, very beginning, the first mention of drinks in the *Outlander* books is the brandy-and-splash—soda water—cocktails served to Claire and Frank in the pub at Inverness. Who could guess what would follow? Rather than keeping things simple, muddled blackberries and lemon make this drink a little bittersweet. Any symbolism regarding the red crushed fruits, bitter rind, thorny brambles, or the brief lives of bubbles is added at your discretion.

Style: **Classic**

4 or 5 FRESH BLACKBERRIES

3 slices LEMON

1½ ounces BRANDY or COGNAC

1 barspoon SIMPLE SYRUP,
or more to taste (page 188)

3 to 4 ounces SODA WATER
for topping

Muddle 3 or 4 of the blackberries and 2 lemon slices in a Collins glass, add the brandy and simple syrup, and stir briefly. Fill the glass with ice and top with the soda water. Garnish with a fresh blackberry and a lemon slice.

Tender Thistle

I F YOU WERE TO see the spiny leaves and tall stems of Scotch thistle (*Onopordum acanthium*, originally native to the Continent), *tender* would not be the word that would come to mind. Yet once trimmed of their spines and cooked, the leaves, stems, and rootstalks of various thistle species have long been eaten in Scotland similarly to the way other cultures have enjoyed that more famous thistle family member, the artichoke. This cocktail employs Cardamaro, an Italian amaro made with two thistle species, cardoon and blessed thistle, and is in honor of those *Outlander* characters— perhaps there's more than one—who maintain a fierce, prickly exterior to the world yet remain tender on the inside.

Style: **Modern**

1 ounce BLENDED SCOTCH

1 ounce CARDAMARO

1 ounce AMONTILLADO SHERRY

1 ounce FRESH APPLE CIDER

¼ ounce ALLSPICE LIQUEUR
or 2 or 3 dashes allspice bitters

FRESH or DRIED THISTLE FLOWER
for garnish

Add all the ingredients to a mixing glass half-filled with ice and stir until chilled. Strain into a chilled cocktail glass and garnish with the thistle flower.

VARIATION: *If a lighter drink is called for, add all the ingredients except the cider to a tall glass and stir, fill with ice, and then top with sparkling cider to taste.*

Freshly Cut Sheaves

YOU CAN'T HAVE WHISKY without harvesting grain. This drink mimics the scent of freshly cut stalks of barley lying in the fields on Fraser's Ridge in autumn by employing barley water, a traditional thirst-quencher popular in Britain but not well known in modern America, along with tropical ingredients to create a light, modern refresher.

Style: **Modern**

1¾ ounces BARLEY WATER
(page 194)

¾ ounce VODKA or GIN
(see note)

¾ ounce FRESHLY SQUEEZED
LEMON JUICE

½ ounce FRESH PINEAPPLE JUICE

½ ounce ORGEAT SYRUP

¼ ounce VANILLA SIMPLE SYRUP
(page 191)

¼ ounce GINGER HONEY SYRUP
(page 190)

POWDERED MATCHA TEA
for garnish

Add all the ingredients to a shaker half-filled with ice. Shake and then strain into a chilled coupe. Garnish with a sprinkle of powdered matcha tea.

NOTE: *While this drink is fine with vodka, it's also an interesting way to use New Western or nontraditional gins, to see how they pair with the fresh, grassy, and lemony flavors here.*

Vintage Coco

YOU MAY OR MAY NOT know that Scotch and coconut water has been a popular drink in the Caribbean for generations. What you should know is that it's an excellent combo; the coconut water brings a touch of sweetness and salinity to the Scotch. Adding more fruit juice and sparkling lime ups the flavor quotient.

Style: 𝕿𝖗𝖔𝖕𝖎𝖈𝖆𝖑

2 ounces COCONUT WATER, or more to taste

½ ounce FRESH PINEAPPLE JUICE

1½ ounces BLENDED SCOTCH

2 ounces FEVER-TREE SPARKLING LIME AND YUZU

SHISO LEAF or MINT SPRIGS for garnish

Add the coconut water, pineapple juice, and Scotch to a highball glass, fill the glass with ice cubes, add the Fever-Tree, and gently stir to mix. Garnish with a shiso leaf or mint sprigs.

Smoke, Grain, and Thistle

DIRTY MARTINIS HAVE HIT a trend in recent years. Shaun Traxler, a bartender at Vault in Fayetteville, Arkansas, had the genius idea of adding Islay Scotch to a Dirty Martini to let the smoky and briny flavors intermingle. This variation ups the vegetal quotient with a measure of Cynar, an amaro made with artichokes, which are in the thistle family. Yes, it's Italian not Scottish, but so's the vermouth. Don't let too much historical dedication get in the way of a good drink!

Style: 𝕸𝖔𝖉𝖊𝖗𝖓

1½ ounces VODKA

1¼ ounces ISLAY PEATED SINGLE MALT SCOTCH, such as Laphroaig

¾ ounce DRY VERMOUTH

¼ ounce CYNAR

1 dash ORANGE BITTERS

1 dash OLIVE BRINE

1 pinch SALT

EXTRA-VIRGIN OLIVE OIL for garnish

Add all the ingredients to a mixing glass half-filled with ice and stir. Strain into a chilled coupe and garnish with a few drops of the olive oil.

Lavender Sachet

WITH A LONG HISTORY of medicinal use for headaches and nervous conditions, as well as serving as an antiseptic and anti-inflammatory, lavender appears in *Outlander* as a remedy, a perfume, and a trigger of memories. Its use in cocktails is more difficult because its strong scent can easily hijack a drink. This recipe is modeled after a classic cocktail, the French 75, named after an artillery piece because of its potent kick—so you've been warned! Lavender is tamed through its inclusion in a honey syrup, but don't ignore the appeal of a fresh or dried lavender sprig as garnish to stimulate the senses.

Style: **Pre-Prohibition**

1½ ounces GIN

½ ounce LAVENDER HONEY SYRUP
(page 191)

½ ounce FRESHLY SQUEEZED
LIME JUICE

¼ teaspoon or less
ORANGE BLOSSOM WATER

CHAMPAGNE or SPARKLING WINE
for topping

LAVENDER SPRIG for garnish

Add all the ingredients to a shaker filled with ice and shake to chill. Strain into a chilled coupe, top with Champagne, and garnish with the lavender sprig.

Chapter

TWO

Spirit-Forward

CONTAINING Thirty-Four Recipes

Pink Linen Gown

THE COSMOPOLITAN IS ONE of those drinks that serious (or overly serious) mixologists like to hate on, but its popularity is undeniable and enduring, and why mess with success? Well, add an ounce or two of Champagne, and this bar standard is transformed into something elegant, refreshing, and as essential to summertime in any century as a pink linen gown.

Style: 𝔐𝔬𝔡𝔢𝔯𝔫

2 slices ORANGE PEEL (see note)

1½ ounces CITRON
or LEMON VODKA

½ ounce FRESHLY SQUEEZED
LIME JUICE

1 ounce 100% CRANBERRY JUICE

¾ ounce COINTREAU
or other orange liqueur

2 ounces CHAMPAGNE for topping

LIME WEDGE for garnish

Add all the ingredients except the Champagne and 1 orange peel to a shaker half-filled with ice and shake. Strain into a chilled coupe and top with the Champagne. Garnish with the remaining orange peel and the lime wedge.

NOTE: *Adding a slice of citrus peel to the shaker before shaking, a technique dubbed "the regal shake" by its creator, sommelier and bartender Theo Lieberman, is a neat way to add some bitter citrus flavor and fragrance to a cocktail without adding extra liquid. Try it in other drinks!*

Penicillin

POSSIBLY THE MOST FAMOUS "new classic" cocktail, this drink was created in the mid-aughts by Sam Ross at the seminal speakeasy cocktail bar Milk & Honey. Its actual health benefits are nil, but in contrast to Claire's home-brewed penicillin in *The Fiery Cross,* it tastes much better. In fact, if made in a mug without ice but with an ounce or two of hot water added, it makes a very restorative hot toddy. This cocktail is also a good starting point for your own experimentation; keep the ratios, but try substituting different base spirits and fruit juices, or use a honey syrup with a different addition like cinnamon or mint for a whole new flavor.

—⁓⁓⁓—

Style: 𝕹𝖊𝖜 𝕮𝖑𝖆𝖘𝖘𝖎𝖈

—⁓⁓⁓—

2 ounces BLENDED SCOTCH

¾ ounce FRESHLY SQUEEZED LEMON JUICE

¾ ounce GINGER HONEY SYRUP (page 190)

½ ounce PEATED SINGLE MALT SCOTCH WHISKY, preferably Laphroaig 10-year

1 piece CANDIED GINGER for garnish

Pour the blended Scotch, lemon juice, and honey syrup into a shaker half-filled with ice and shake until chilled. Strain into a rocks glass with 1 large ice cube. Slowly pour the peated Scotch whisky over the back of a spoon into the drink, and garnish with the candied ginger.

Flintlock Pistol

FROM THE MARSHES of Prestonpans to the North Carolina Piedmont, the flintlock pistol was the standard sidearm of the eighteenth century. By the middle of the next century, the revolver had taken its place. So when Bay Area bartender Jon Santer invented a drink in the early aughts made of Bulleit bourbon with a flamed orange peel garnish creating a puff like gun smoke, he named it the Revolver, naturally. Turning back the clock on this drink involves splitting the base between bourbon (Bulleit or another brand) and Scotch. Using crème de cacao as well as coffee liqueur darkens the flavor, as befits the greater smokiness of the earlier weapon.

—⁓⁓⁓—

Style: 𝕸𝖔𝖉𝖊𝖗𝖓

—⁓⁓⁓—

1 ounce BOURBON

1 ounce BLENDED MALT SCOTCH
(see note)

¼ ounce COFFEE LIQUEUR

¼ ounce CRÈME DE CACAO

2 dashes ORANGE BITTERS

Wide slice ORANGE PEEL
for garnish (see note)

Combine all the ingredients in a mixing glass half-filled with ice and stir until chilled. Strain into a chilled coupe and garnish with the orange peel.

NOTES: *Choose a Scotch with some peat influence for this recipe, or use an Islay single malt for full-bore flavor. A bottled in bond or cask-strength bourbon is similarly recommended.*

To flame the orange peel, cut a large, wide slice of peel, light a wooden match, and position the peel with one hand so that, when squeezed, the expressed oils shoot through the flame before landing on the surface of the drink. Drop the expressed peel into the drink. This technique is particularly dramatic under low light!

The Wildest Redhead

H OW COULD WE NOT include a drink with this name, especially when it's a modern classic-in-the-making Scotch whisky cocktail, full of honey and spice notes, by renowned New York bartender Meaghan Dorman, who is, in fact, red-haired.

—⌁⌁⌁—

Style: 𝕹𝖊𝖜 𝕮𝖑𝖆𝖘𝖘𝖎𝖈

—⌁⌁⌁—

1½ ounces BLENDED SCOTCH

¾ ounce FRESHLY SQUEEZED LEMON JUICE

½ ounce RICH HONEY SYRUP (page 192)

¼ ounce ALLSPICE DRAM

¼ ounce CHERRY BRANDY

Combine all the ingredients except the cherry brandy in a cocktail shaker half-filled with ice and shake until chilled. Strain into a rocks glass with one large ice cube. Slowly pour the cherry brandy over the back of a spoon into the glass so it floats on top.

Collecting the Rents

C LAIRE WAS INVITED INTO a crofter's cottage for a refreshing drink
of cider during her trip collecting rents with Jamie and the MacKenzies.
This long cider drink amplifies the refreshment with a split base of Scotch
and apple brandy. Use fresh local cider if it's available.

Style: 𝕸𝖔𝖉𝖊𝖗𝖓

1 ounce BLENDED SCOTCH,
such as The Sassenach

1 ounce APPLE BRANDY

¾ ounce FRESHLY SQUEEZED
LEMON JUICE

2 ounces FRESH APPLE CIDER

FRESHLY GROUND CINNAMON
for garnish

1 small CINNAMON STICK
for garnish

1 slice LEMON
for garnish

Fill a tall glass with ice cubes, add all the
ingredients, and stir to combine. Sprinkle
a small amount of the ground cinnamon
on top, and garnish with the cinnamon
stick and lemon slice.

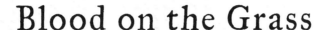

Blood on the Grass

THERE ARE MANY BATTLES in *Outlander*, from large armies warring over the fate of nations to smaller, though no less violent, encounters. As such, this is less a specific recipe than a template, the signature technique of which is the small amount of bright red Campari that is poured slowly down the side of the cocktail glass so that it sinks to the bottom. Those with memories of drinking in the 1970s and 1980s may recall the Tequila Sunrise, which used this technique with grenadine.

Built with overproof rum, amaro, lime juice, and simple syrup, this drink packs a real punch, appropriately given its name. The Campari provides a bittersweet finish, making it a good drink to serve before dinner. Make it with gin, and the drink becomes more botanical, more like a Negroni. As you gain more experience with it, you can also try other spirits, other citrus, and other amari for a bloody cornucopia of flavors, as Claire might say.

— ⁓⁓⁓⁓ —

Style: 𝕸𝖔𝖉𝖊𝖗𝖓

— ⁓⁓⁓⁓ —

2 ounces WHITE OVERPROOF RUM

½ ounce FRESHLY SQUEEZED LIME JUICE

½ ounce SIMPLE SYRUP (page 188)

¼ ounce CIOCIARO AMARO or other bitter orange–flavored amaro

½ ounce CAMPARI

Add all the ingredients except the Campari to a shaker half-filled with ice and shake to chill. Strain into a chilled coupe and "sink" the Campari by pouring it slowly down the side of the glass.

Cameron's Kick

THIS DRINK HAS NO connection to Aunt Jocasta; it's a "lost classic" created by Scottish bartender Harry MacElhone, founder of the celebrated Harry's New York Bar in Paris in the 1920s. It's also a simple yet delightful early example of a split-base cocktail, being made with both Scotch and Irish whiskey, along with orgeat syrup, an almond syrup seen more often these days in tropical drinks or caffeinated frappes. Who is this Cameron and who or what was he kicking? No one knows, so we are free to imagine a wayward descendant of the Cameron clan finding work in Paris and inspiring Mr. MacElhone. And the rest, as they say, is history.

Style: **Pre-Prohibition**

1 ounce BLENDED SCOTCH

1 ounce BLENDED IRISH WHISKEY

¾ ounce FRESHLY SQUEEZED LEMON JUICE

½ ounce ORGEAT SYRUP

Add all the ingredients to a shaker half-filled with ice and shake, then strain into a chilled coupe.

Annie Bos

ANNIE BOS IS NOT a character from *Outlander*. She was an actress who became the Netherlands' first silent film diva. Retiring in the 1920s, she never spoke a word out loud on camera. In the *Outlander* episode "Famous Last Words," Roger MacKenzie's hanging is depicted in eerie silent black-and-white film style. This cocktail by Edinburgh bartender Iain McPherson manages to connect early film history with the postmodern approach of season five's cinematography through the magic of a single malt genever brewed in Schiedam at a distiller owned by a family that has been in the business since 1777, almost to the exact time of the Battle of Alamance in North Carolina.

Style: 𝔐𝔬𝔡𝔢𝔯𝔫

1 ounce OLD DUFF 100% MALT WINE
GENEVER GIN

1 ounce FRESHLY SQUEEZED
LEMON JUICE

1 ounce NIXTA LICOR DE ELOTE
(corn liqueur)

⅓ ounce SIMPLE SYRUP
(page 188)

1 slice LEMON
for garnish

Shake all the ingredients in a shaker filled with ice. Fine-strain into a chilled coupe glass. Garnish with a lemon coin squeezed over the drink and dropped in.

Bitter Cascara

BITTER CASCARA, ALSO KNOWN as cascara sagrada, is the bark from an American buckthorn tree species. The mysterious French apothecary Raymond uses bitter cascara in fake "poisons" sold to the Vicomtesse de Rambeau (*Dragonfly in Amber*). On its own, cascara is indeed unpleasantly bitter. Recently, some American distillers have added it to their products for the same reason bitter herbs such as gentian and wormwood are added to vermouths and amari: a small amount provides a pleasant bitterness that is supposed to be good for digestion. Try this Negroni Bianco variant before dinner.

Style: 𝕸𝖔𝖉𝖊𝖗𝖓

1½ ounces AMASS DRY GIN
(see note)

1½ ounces ST. GEORGE BRUTO
AMERICANO (see note)

1½ ounces DRY VERMOUTH

1 LEMON PEEL for garnish

Combine all the ingredients in a mixing glass half-filled with ice and stir until chilled. Strain into a chilled cocktail glass. Twist the lemon peel to express the oils over the drink and add to the glass.

NOTE: *Both the gin and the Americano specified here are made with cascara. If you don't have or can't find Amass dry gin, substitute a good London dry gin—or better yet, a New Western gin. For the Bruto Americano, substitute Suze or another French bitter liqueur. Do not attempt to make it with cascara sagrada tea or supplements, which have not been approved by the FDA.*

Bobby Burns

ONE OF THE FEW pre-Prohibition classic Scotch-based cocktails, this drink is essentially a Manhattan variation, with added honey-herbal depth from Bénédictine. And like the Manhattan, the measurements may be adjusted to emphasize one of the ingredients. This version is strong and centered on the Scotch, as befits a drink named after Scotland's national poet. (You need a Scotch with some heft to it to stand up to the other ingredients.) Withholding this recipe from a cocktail book that riffs on Scottish history would perhaps not be technically illegal, but it would be deeply dishonorable all the same.

— ᨜᨜᨜᨜ —

Style: 𝕻𝖗𝖊-𝕻𝖗𝖔𝖍𝖎𝖇𝖎𝖙𝖎𝖔𝖓

— ᨜᨜᨜᨜ —

2 ounces BLENDED MALT SCOTCH
or single malt

¾ ounce SWEET VERMOUTH

¼ ounce BÉNÉDICTINE

LEMON PEEL
for garnish

Stir all the ingredients in a mixing glass half-filled with ice and strain into a chilled coupe. Twist the lemon peel over the drink to express the oils and drop it in.

Famous Nudity

L ET'S BE HONEST: the steamy sex scenes are part of what's made the *Outlander* books and series famous—perhaps also because they are frequently told or shot from the female point of view. This drink is a variation of a new classic called the Naked and Famous, which itself was a riff on another new classic, the Paper Plane, which was based on a pre-Prohibition classic called the Last Word. Yes, cocktails have family trees, too. There are no historical ingredients here, just a perfect balance between smoky mezcal, spice, and fruit flavors from the liqueurs and the sweetness of pineapple. Try it and see what mood it gets you into.

Style: 𝕸𝖔𝖉𝖊𝖗𝖓

1 ounce MEZCAL

½ ounce APEROL

½ ounce YELLOW CHARTREUSE

¾ ounce FRESHLY SQUEEZED LIME JUICE

1 ounce FRESH PINEAPPLE JUICE

2 dashes CACAO BITTERS

PINEAPPLE FROND and/or slice of fresh pineapple for garnish

Shake all the ingredients together with ice, then strain into a brandy snifter or Old-Fashioned glass filled with crushed ice. Garnish with a pineapple frond and/ or a slice of pineapple.

Up the Hudson

A GENEVER-BASED MANHATTAN, this drink is boozy yet with balanced sweetness. It commemorates Claire and Jamie's unwilling passage on board the privateer *Asp* past the island of Manhattan—a place where much genever was consumed in colonial times—on their way up the river to Fort Ticonderoga in *An Echo in the Bone.* The bitters employed here, Peychaud's, come from a city on another river, namely New Orleans, but their licorice and fruit flavors work especially well with genever. Incidentally, they were invented by an apothecary, Antoine Peychaud, who fled to America after the successful revolution by enslaved Africans on the island known as Hispaniola, modern-day Haiti and the Dominican Republic, the scene of another of Jamie and Claire's many voyages.

Style: **Pre-Prohibition**

2 ounces GENEVER, such as Old Duff

1 ounce SWEET VERMOUTH

½ ounce CHERRY BRANDY

1 barspoon DEMERARA SYRUP

2 dashes PEYCHAUD'S BITTERS

FRESH or COCKTAIL CHERRY
for garnish

Combine all the ingredients in a mixing glass half-filled with ice. Strain into a chilled coupe. Garnish with the cherry.

Angelus Bells

A "BELL-RINGER" WAS A STYLE of cocktail invented around 1900, which involved serving the drink in a glass coated with apricot brandy. This one references Claire's hearing the Angelus bells ringing at the Abbey of Saint Anne in Le Havre (in *Dragonfly in Amber*) and so employs French ingredients to create a drink with grace and high style.

Style: **Pre-Prohibition**

⅙ ounce APRICOT BRANDY
for rinsing

1½ ounces LONDON DRY GIN

½ ounce COGNAC

½ ounce BÉNÉDICTINE

½ ounce FRESHLY SQUEEZED
LEMON JUICE

¼ ounce RICH SIMPLE SYRUP
(page 188)

1 dash ORANGE BITTERS

1 dash ANGOSTURA BITTERS

First rinse a chilled cocktail or rocks glass by swirling the apricot brandy around to coat the inside; discard any excess. Combine all the other ingredients in a cocktail shaker with ice and shake until chilled. Strain into the glass.

VARIATION: *Omit the rinse and just add the apricot brandy along with the other ingredients, then strain this cocktail into a tall glass filled with ice. Top it with an ounce or two of soda water and you'll convert it into a Sling, a classic style of warm-weather drink. Bell-Ringer Slinger, anyone?*

Coffee and Corn

WHERE WOULD A COLONIAL homesteader, or a surgeon, be without coffee? Whether it's ground in a quern on the Ridge or snagged in a cup from the local shop, it's a necessity for Claire and many others. High-quality small-batch coffee liqueurs have raised the game in bartenders' circles recently, and they're powering up everything from the Espresso Martini to more unusual combinations like this one. There are multiple puns involved as well: coffee is coffee, of course, but the patent still that revolutionized distilling in the mid-nineteenth century was called the Coffey still. And corn, in the colonial period, especially in the British Isles, meant any sort of grain, including barley, not just Native American maize.

Style: **Modern**

1½ ounces BLENDED MALT SCOTCH

½ ounce CIOCIARO AMARO

½ ounce COFFEE LIQUEUR

1 dash ORANGE BITTERS

1 dash CACAO BITTERS

1 ORANGE PEEL and 1 ESPRESSO BEAN for garnish

Add all the ingredients to a mixing glass half-filled with ice, stir, and strain into a chilled coupe. Garnish with the orange peel and espresso bean.

Stone Circle

THE ORIGINS OF THE stones at Craigh na Dun and their magic remain mysterious, but the stones are an essential part of the story. They serve as a metaphor for the "pull" of love despite the distances of time and space, the desire to find home, and that special family—the Frasers—who endure over the convoluted course of several centuries. Glasgow bartender Jack Jamieson created this Stone Circle based on the Manhattan, an ur-cocktail if ever there was one, whose exact origins are also shrouded in mystery.

Style: 𝔐𝔬𝔡𝔢𝔯𝔫

1 ounce PEATED SINGLE MALT SCOTCH WHISKY

1 ounce RYE WHISKEY

1 ounce SWEET VERMOUTH

½ ounce GLAYVA (see note)

2 dashes CHOCOLATE BITTERS

2 dashes PEYCHAUD'S BITTERS

1 wide ORANGE PEEL for garnish

Add all the ingredients to a mixing glass half-filled with ice and stir. Add a large ice cube to a rocks glass and strain the drink over the ice cube. Flame the orange peel over the drink (see note on page 62 for flaming the citrus peel).

NOTE: *Glayva, very popular in Scotland, is a whisky liqueur flavored with tangerine, honey, and spices. If it's not available near you, try muddling a section of fresh tangerine in the mixing glass before adding the other ingredients, and consider substituting another liqueur with a similar profile, such as Bénédictine or dry curaçao.*

The Spice Bribe

CLAIRE NEEDED TO USE a bundle of expensive spices to bribe the cook of the *Porpoise* to give her boiling water during Jamie's bout with seasickness. This drink is a veritable spice rack between the Meletti, an amaro flavored with saffron and violets; the Chartreuse; the bitters; and the spicy flavor of rye. It is not a cure for nausea but may very well keep you out of the doldrums.

—~~~~~—

Style: 𝕸𝖔𝖉𝖊𝖗𝖓

—~~~~~—

1 ounce RYE WHISKEY,
preferably bottled in bond

1 ounce MELETTI

1 teaspoon GREEN CHARTREUSE

1 teaspoon VANILLA SIMPLE SYRUP
(page 191)

1 dash ANGOSTURA BITTERS

1 dash ORANGE BITTERS

1 wide ORANGE PEEL for garnish

Add all the ingredients to a mixing glass half-filled with ice and stir, then strain into a chilled rocks glass with 1 large ice cube. Garnish with the orange peel.

Scottish Festival

THIS ONE'S A BIT tricky to place. In *Drums of Autumn,* the Scottish festival takes place in New England; in the TV series, it's in the mountains of North Carolina and it's 1969. So what would people have been drinking while watching the games and listening to the music? Best guess would be cheap blended Scotch, which might have been mixed with all sorts of things. This mixture, whether historically accurate or not, is easy sipping.

Style: 𝕸𝖔𝖉𝖊𝖗𝖓

2 ounces BLENDED SCOTCH WHISKY, or substitute bourbon if you're feeling Southern

¾ ounce FRESHLY SQUEEZED LEMON JUICE

¾ ounce PURE MAPLE SYRUP

2 or 3 dashes ANGOSTURA BITTERS

Add all the ingredients to a mixing glass half-filled with ice and stir until chilled. Strain into a chilled rocks glass with a single large ice cube, or dump the ice and liquid into a plastic cup to go.

Peat's Dragon

CREATED BY BAHAMAS BAR owner Kyle Jones, the Peat's Dragon makes a great introduction to mezcal, if you're a Scotch lover who hasn't yet crossed over to that other smoky distillate, and a fine example of the use of peat-heavy Scotch as one among several flavor elements. The passengers and crew of the *Porpoise* met no dragons as they passed by the Bahamas, stopping only to take on fresh water. But they would have appreciated this drink.

Style: 𝔐𝔬𝔡𝔢𝔯𝔫

1½ ounces ISLAY PEATED SINGLE
MALT SCOTCH

1 ounce MEZCAL

½ ounce FINO SHERRY

½ ounce AGAVE SYRUP

¼ ounce FRESHLY SQUEEZED
LEMON JUICE

1 DEHYDRATED LEMON WHEEL
for garnish

Shake all the ingredients with ice in a cocktail shaker and strain into a chilled rocks glass filled with ice. Garnish with the dehydrated lemon wheel.

Ruby Port and a Fine Cheroot

LORD JOHN GREY, along with other upper-class characters, was known to indulge in a cheroot, or cigar, on occasion; frequently after dinner with a glass of something alcoholic. That combination of flavors is mimicked by a new classic cocktail named 100-Year-Old Cigar, which employs absinthe to rinse the glass into which the cocktail is poured. Since absinthe wasn't a thing until the mid-nineteenth century, this cocktail uses a float of ruby port to evoke the more historically accurate pairing.

Style: 𝔐𝔬𝔡𝔢𝔯𝔫

1¾ ounces AGED RUM (use a long-aged rum, preferably pot-still)

½ ounce CYNAR

½ ounce BÉNÉDICTINE

¼ ounce PEATED SCOTCH

1 dash ANGOSTURA BITTERS

½ ounce RUBY PORT

Add all the ingredients except the port to a mixing glass half-filled with ice and stir. Strain into a chilled coupe. Introduce the port by slowly pouring it over the back of a spoon, floating it onto the surface of the drink.

Sgian-Dubh

THE *SGIAN-DUBH,* AKA THE "Black Blade," was a small dagger worn inside the sock as part of the traditional Highlander outfit. This drink is a riff on the Black Manhattan, itself a variant of the classic cocktail that replaces the vermouth with a dark, rich amaro.

Style: 𝕸𝖔𝖉𝖊𝖗𝖓

1 ounce BLENDED SCOTCH,
such as The Sassenach

1 ounce ISLAY PEATED SINGLE
MALT SCOTCH,
such as Laphroaig

1 ounce AVERNA AMARO

1 dash ORANGE BITTERS

1 dash ANGOSTURA BITTERS

1 COCKTAIL CHERRY for garnish

Pour all the ingredients into a mixing glass half-filled with ice and stir until chilled. Strain into a chilled cocktail glass and garnish with the cherry.

Moonlight on Stone

MOONLIGHT IS HARD TO describe in print. Is it white? Is it silver? Is it tinged with color? Whatever shade you choose, it's hard to imagine the standing stones of Craigh na Dun in any other light. Evoking moonlight in a cocktail is similarly challenging, but it has been attempted. The late Gaz Regan, one of the godfathers of the modern cocktail renaissance, created one called the Moonlight Cocktail, which itself riffed on a pre-Prohibition classic called the Aviation. Both recipes used a violet-colored and -flavored liqueur, crème de violette, to evoke the sky. This liqueur, like Crème Yvette (page 91), though very popular around the turn of the twentieth century, is often too sweet and perfumed for modern tastes. Hence, this version uses a mere whisper of it to accentuate the floral and citrus notes of this drink.

Style: **Pre-Prohibition**

1½ ounces LONDON DRY GIN

½ ounce DRY CURAÇAO
or other orange liqueur

1 ounce FRESHLY SQUEEZED
LIME JUICE

¼ ounce SIMPLE SYRUP
(page 188)

1 barspoon CRÈME DE VIOLETTE
(feel free to experiment with more,
but go easy)

2 dashes ORANGE BITTERS

Add all the ingredients to a shaker half-filled with ice and shake. Strain into a chilled coupe and drink by moonlight or other suitable illumination.

Tricorn Hat

T HE TRICORN HAT WAS the latest in men's fashion during the mid-1700s in Europe and its colonies and was particularly sharp-looking when worn with powdered or pomaded hair pulled back into a long queue. This fashion statement drink begins with a liquid historical classic, the Trilby No. 2, which dates back to the end of the nineteenth century and shared some of the genetic makeup of the Manhattan, being made with either Scotch whisky or Old Tom gin and red, aka sweet, vermouth. Its signature ingredient, however, was Crème Yvette, a violet-and-berry-flavored liqueur that tends to turn alcoholic drinks into something like grandmother's hand soap if used to excess. The Tricorn dispenses with such frippery, being made with yellow Chartreuse for a less lurid color and more understated taste. Enjoy it with your hat on or off.

Style: **Pre-Prohibition**

1½ ounces BLENDED SCOTCH

¾ ounce SWEET VERMOUTH

¼ ounce YELLOW CHARTREUSE

2 dashes ORANGE BITTERS

1 ORANGE PEEL for garnish

Add all the ingredients to a mixing glass half-filled with ice and stir. Strain into a chilled coupe and garnish with the orange peel.

White Oak Propeller

THIS DRINK IS A variation of the Paper Plane, another new classic cocktail by NYC bartender Sam Ross. White oak was actually used to make propellers and other aircraft parts all the way up through World War II, so it's probable that Claire or Frank saw wooden, not paper, planes in action during their wartime service. The other connection is the use of barrel-aged Old Tom gin, that historic nineteenth-century style of gin, with roots all the way back to early-eighteenth-century–flavored genevers and gins based on Scotch whisky distillates that were shipped and stored in white oak barrels. (It must be a barrel-aged gin—Barr Hill and Ransom both make excellent choices.) You can also just enjoy this drink without all the historical details about old rotgut. It's way smoother.

Style: 𝕸𝖔𝖉𝖊𝖗𝖓

¾ ounce OLD TOM GIN

¾ ounce BIANCO VERMOUTH

¾ ounce AMARO NONINO

¾ ounce APEROL

Add all the ingredients to a cocktail mixer half-filled with ice and shake well until chilled. Strain into a chilled cocktail glass.

Sazerach

J ACK JAMIESON'S GLASGOW UPDATE of the classic New Orleans
cocktail the Sazerac is named after everyone's favorite Sassenach, who's
been known to enjoy a dram or two of whisky.

Style: **Pre-Prohibition**

2¼ ounces LIGHTLY PEATED
HIGHLAND SINGLE MALT
SCOTCH WHISKY

¼ ounce TABLET SYRUP
(see note)

3 dashes PEYCHAUD'S BITTERS

1 dash PIMENTO BITTERS
or allspice liqueur

1 barspoon ABSINTHE

Combine all the ingredients but the
absinthe in a mixing glass and stir over
ice. Rinse a chilled rocks glass with
absinthe and strain the cocktail into the
prepared glass.

NOTE: *Tablet is a traditional Scottish fudgelike
dessert made with condensed milk, sugar, and
butter. To make tablet syrup, combine 2 ounces
tablet, ½ cup brown sugar, and ½ cup water
in a pot. Heat and stir until the tablet has
dissolved and then strain it into a bottle. Keep
in the fridge. If you don't have tablet available
or don't want to make it from scratch, you can
substitute butterscotch or dulce de leche thinned
out with an equal amount of water; the taste
won't be as authentic, but it will be close.*

Chess and Conversation

THE DINNERS BETWEEN Lord John Grey and Jamie in Ardsmuir Prison involve more than a literal chess game, as each man tries to find out more about the other and they begin to establish their friendship despite the circumstances. Fine Scotch, sherry, and an unusual tincture create a complex combination that is worth savoring slowly as you ponder your next move.

Style: 𝕸𝖔𝖉𝖊𝖗𝖓

1½ ounces BLENDED MALT SCOTCH,
or splurge on a
sherry-finished single malt

¾ ounce AMONTILLADO SHERRY

½ ounce DRY VERMOUTH

½ ounce BIANCO VERMOUTH

2 dashes ANGOSTURA BITTERS

1 dash ORANGE BITTERS

1 dash TOASTED COCONUT
TINCTURE (page 195)

1 ORANGE PEEL for garnish

Add all the ingredients to a mixing glass half-filled with ice and stir. Strain into a chilled coupe and garnish with the orange peel.

Tryst

HERE ARE SO MANY secret meetings between lovers in *Outlander* that it makes little sense to single one out. Instead, just enjoy this Whisky Sour variation by Jack Jamieson, made with high-quality Cognac—surely a spirit that signals romance—for your own next rendezvous. Don't tell anyone what happens.

Style: 𝕸𝖔𝖉𝖊𝖗𝖓

1 ounce SPEYSIDE SINGLE MALT WHISKY

1 ounce VSOP COGNAC

1 ounce COINTREAU or other slightly sweeter Triple Sec

¾ ounce FRESHLY SQUEEZED LEMON JUICE

Add all the ingredients to a shaker over ice, shake, and strain into a chilled coupe.

The Big Man

NAMED FOR THE Big Man himself, Jamie Fraser, this concoction by Jack Jamieson employs raspberry syrup for the requisite red color. It also uses the sweeter style of French vermouth, known as bianco or blanc. Because the flavor profile of bianco vermouths varies considerably from brand to brand, taste yours first and adjust the amount, if necessary, so it plays nicely with the whisky rather than fighting each other, as Jamie and Claire tend to from time to time. If available, a sprig of raspberry leaves for garnish adds color and recalls Claire's treatment of Jamie's injured hand with these same leaves.

Style: 𝕸𝖔𝖉𝖊𝖗𝖓

1¾ ounces CAMPBELTOWN SINGLE MALT WHISKY

1 ounce BIANCO VERMOUTH

½ ounce DRY CURAÇAO

1 barspoon RASPBERRY SYRUP (page 191)

1 RASPBERRY and/or
1 RASPBERRY LEAF for garnish

Add all the ingredients to a mixing glass and stir down over ice. Strain into a chilled coupe and garnish with the fresh raspberry and/or raspberry leaf.

Brothel Brunch

THERE IS UNEXPECTED CAMARADERIE between Claire and the prostitutes at Madame Jeanne's, and together they find the simple joy of breakfast after a long night. This drink features grapefruit, lemon, passion fruit, and an egg white, so it's the perfect pick-me-up. You can substitute a citrus-flavored apéritif such as Cocchi Americano or Lillet Blanc for the L'aperitivo Nonino.

Style: **Modern**

¾ ounce LONDON DRY GIN

¾ ounce APEROL

¾ ounce L'APERITIVO NONINO

¾ ounce FRESHLY SQUEEZED
LEMON JUICE

½ ounce PASSION FRUIT SYRUP

¼ ounce AGAVE SYRUP

1 dash GRAPEFRUIT BITTERS

1 EGG WHITE or 1 dash vegan foamer

Add all the ingredients to a shaker and dry-shake without ice. Add ice and shake to chill. Double-strain into a chilled coupe.

Any Last Words

L AST WORDS BEFORE PARTING. Last words before dying. Last words before . . . is it ever really the end? Fans may hope the words keep coming in the form of new books and shows. Jack Jamieson's creation here is another riff on the Last Word, a pre-Prohibition classic that has inspired any number of variations, with no end in sight. If you don't have any oak chips handy or are reluctant to start an open fire in your home, view the note below for possible substitutes. Or dispense with the smoking entirely, although the smoky swirl as it disappears into thin air gives a fine sense of finality.

Style: 𝕸𝖔𝖉𝖊𝖗𝖓

1 ounce PEATED SINGLE MALT
SCOTCH WHISKY

1 ounce GREEN CHARTREUSE

1 ounce LUXARDO MARASCHINO
ORIGINALE

1 ounce FRESHLY SQUEEZED
LIME JUICE

OAK WOOD CHIPS
for smoking (see note)

Shake all the ingredients over ice. Place some oak chips on a flameproof surface, ignite them, and let them burn for a few moments; then blow them out and put a coupe glass next to the smoking chips. Place a smoking cloche (or glass baking bowl or other domed vessel) over the top and let it fill with oak smoke. Leave for 2 minutes before lifting the cloche off in a circular manner to swirl the smoke. Strain the cocktail into the smoked glass.

NOTE: *An alternative to smoking wood chips would be a dash of any bitters made with a smoked chile or other "smoked" element on top of the finished drink. You might even get away with a sprinkle of smoked paprika, which would add an interesting color and texture!*

The Bonnie Prince's Consolation

WHILE PRINCE CHARLES STUART is credited with giving the recipe for Drambuie to the MacKinnon family for helping him escape after the Battle of Culloden, there's not much evidence of what he actually drank. Raised in Rome and exiled to various parts of Europe after the failed uprising, it's likely the prince had cosmopolitan tastes, shaped in part by the financial insecurity of being a man without a country. This cocktail combines ingredients from different countries: gin from Scotland, calvados from France, and vermouth from Italy, along with pan-European apricot brandy to make a sophisticated yet soothing sipper.

Style: 𝕸𝖔𝖉𝖊𝖗𝖓

¾ ounce BARREL-AGED GIN

¾ ounce CALVADOS

1½ ounces DRY VERMOUTH

¼ ounce APRICOT BRANDY

1 long strip of ORANGE PEEL

1 thin APPLE SLICE for garnish

1 DRIED APRICOT for garnish

Add all the ingredients to a mixing glass half-filled with ice and shake. Strain into a chilled coupe. Garnish with the apple slice and dried apricot skewered with a toothpick or placed on the glass rim.

Jesus H. Roosevelt Christ Swizzle

NAMED AFTER CLAIRE'S signature swear phrase, this drink actually connects to FDR himself, who enjoyed more than a few swizzles on the frequent boat cruises he took to improve his health during his presidency. With 3 full ounces of rum, this is not a juice cleanse, but you may end up swearing out of pure delighted surprise. Like many tropical-style drinks, it relies on more than one type of rum to create a complex flavor, while the swizzle technique stirs and cools the liquid without undue dilution.

Style: **Tropical**

1½ ounces AGED DARK RUM
(or refine the flavor by using a
long-aged pot-still rum)

1½ ounces AGED GOLD RUM

1 ounce FRESH PINEAPPLE JUICE

1 ounce FRESHLY SQUEEZED
LIME JUICE

1 ounce VELVET FALERNUM (a sweet
liqueur flavored with lime, clove, and ginger,
essential for many tropical drinks)

3 dashes ANGOSTURA BITTERS

3 dashes HERBSAINT (or substitute another
anise-flavored spirit like Ricard or absinthe)

1 slice LIME or PINEAPPLE
for garnish

Add all the ingredients to a tall glass and fill with crushed ice. Using a swizzle stick or a long barspoon, swizzle the drink by placing the spoon down to the bottom of the glass then twirling it between your palms as you pull up toward the top of the drink and back down. Fill with more crushed ice if needed, and garnish with the slice of lime or pineapple—or even a cocktail cherry, a paper umbrella, plastic porpoise, toy boat, or what have you.

Fraises de Bois de Fraser

THERE'S POWERFUL SYMBOLISM in strawberries, prominently featured in the Fraser clan's coat of arms—in fact, historians tell us the family name came from "fraises," the French word for strawberries. Jamie explains all this to Claire: "The white flowers are for honor, and red fruit for courage—and the green leaves are for constancy." This recipe, based on the classic Lemon Drop, employs basil leaves instead of strawberry leaves to elevate the formula beyond the ordinary.

Style: 𝕸𝖔𝖉𝖊𝖗𝖓

2 ounces VODKA

½ ounce ORANGE CURAÇAO

½ ounce STRAWBERRY BASIL SYRUP
(page 192)

1 ounce FRESHLY SQUEEZED
LEMON JUICE

1 FRESH BASIL LEAF for garnish

Add all the ingredients to a shaker half-filled with ice, shake, and strain into a chilled coupe. Garnish with the fresh basil leaf.

Fiery Redhead

DOES THIS EVEN NEED an introduction? It's a modern creation from Jack Jamieson, featuring a double dose of sherry in both the whisky finish and as a separate ingredient. East India sherry refers to a historic practice of aging sherry by shipping casks of it all the way to the East Indies and back. The current Lustau version does not go to sea, but aging in a hot, humid location results in a rich complexity and tanginess that perfectly suits a fiery redhead who fell for an equally salty lass with eyes like whisky with the sun shining behind it.

Style: 𝕸𝖔𝖉𝖊𝖗𝖓

2 ounces DALMORE 12 WHISKY
(can be subbed for another
sherried Highland malt)

⅔ ounce LUSTAU EAST INDIA
SOLERA SHERRY

¼ ounce GINGER LIQUEUR

2 dashes CHOCOLATE BITTERS

ORANGE PEEL and
MARASCHINO CHERRY for garnish

Add all the ingredients to a mixing glass over ice. Stir and strain into a chilled coupe. Garnish with the orange peel and maraschino cherry.

Offal Old-Fashioned

A N EARLY STAR OF the current cocktail revival was the Benton's Old-Fashioned, created at pioneering NYC speakeasy PDT. It featured the unusual ingredient of bourbon infused—or "fat-washed"—with bacon. This Scottish rendition by Jack Jamieson employs the somewhat controversial cornerstone of its traditional cuisine, haggis—the innards (or heart, lungs, and liver) of a lamb mixed with oatmeal, seasoned with spices, stuffed into a sheep's stomach, and boiled. If haggis turns you off (Lord John Grey himself sent it back and asked for mutton instead), use another fat-washed whisky to a similar effect.

—〜〜〜—

Style: 𝕸𝖔𝖉𝖊𝖗𝖓

—〜〜〜—

2½ ounces HAGGIS-WASHED WHISKY (see recipe at right)

½ ounce BLACK PEPPER HONEY SYRUP (page 188)

3 dashes ANGOSTURA BITTERS

1 ORANGE PEEL for garnish

SCOTTISH SHORTBREAD for serving

Add all the ingredients to a mixing glass half-filled with ice and stir. Add a large cube of ice to a rocks glass and strain the drink into the glass. Garnish with the orange peel and serve with a piece of shortbread on the side.

To make the haggis-washed whisky, grill or broil ¼ pound haggis until it begins to crisp up. Add it to a jar along with 4 ounces of blended whisky. Seal the jar and leave it to infuse in the fridge for 1 week. Strain through a fine-mesh sieve or cheesecloth.

Chapter

THREE

—— ////// ——

After Dinner and Dessert

CONTAINING Sixteen Recipes

Crème de Menthe Coffin

WHILE THE IMAGE of a dead body stashed in a cask of crème de menthe in *Voyager* may have single-handedly lowered global sales of this classic liqueur, there's no reason to forswear minty drinks forever. The Stinger, a pre-Prohibition brandy and crème de menthe cocktail, has been tinkered with in recent years and serves as the basis for this offering that doesn't drown the brandy, so to speak, but augments it with a minty amaro and the potent allure of absinthe. Note: Using green crème de menthe instead of white will not change the flavor but will result in a greenish-brown hue that may not be quite as appetizing.

Style: 𝕸𝖔𝖉𝖊𝖗𝖓

1½ ounces COGNAC

½ ounce CRÈME DE MENTHE

¼ ounce BRANCA MENTA

1 or 2 dashes ABSINTHE

Sprig of FRESH MINT for garnish

Combine all the ingredients except the absinthe in a mixing glass half-filled with ice and stir. Dash the absinthe into a chilled rocks glass and roll the glass to coat the sides, discarding any excess. Strain the drink into the prepared glass and garnish with the sprig of fresh mint.

Drums of Autumn

APPLES AND BAKING SPICE, burning leaves and woodsmoke, sweetness tinged with melancholy for the departing warm weather—these impressions of the fall season are mingled in a glass, perfect for relaxing after dinner by a fire. Keep in mind these are potent ingredients, so stir well to provide some dilution, and don't rush the sipping!

Style: 𝕸𝖔𝖉𝖊𝖗𝖓

1 ounce RYE WHISKEY
(use an overproof rye if available)

1 ounce CALVADOS

1 ounce SWEET VERMOUTH

¼ ounce GREEN CHARTREUSE

2 dashes ANGOSTURA BITTERS

1 barspoon ISLAY PEATED SINGLE MALT SCOTCH

1 wide ORANGE PEEL,
flamed, for garnish

Add all the ingredients except the single malt to a mixing glass half-filled with ice and stir to chill. Strain into a chilled rocks glass with 1 large ice cube. Float the Scotch over the top of the drink by pouring it slowly over the back of a spoon held just above the surface of the drink. Garnish with the flamed orange peel (see note on page 62).

Lion Rampant

THE NAME OF THIS cocktail is one of the traditional heraldic symbols of the Scottish royal family and is still displayed at public events today. The lion this cocktail by Jack Jamieson refers to might also be the Lion's Tail, a bourbon cocktail, here made more Gaelic with Scotch whisky and birch water syrup. The latter is an unusual ingredient, but one with a long history of use in drinks and as a flavoring in both Scotland and North America.

Style: 𝕸𝖔𝖉𝖊𝖗𝖓

2 ounces BLENDED SCOTCH WHISKY

¾ ounce ALLSPICE DRAM LIQUEUR

½ ounce BIRCH WATER SYRUP
(page 188)

¾ ounce FRESHLY SQUEEZED
LEMON JUICE

1 EGG WHITE or
1 dash vegan foamer

1 piece CRYSTALLIZED GINGER
for garnish

Add all the ingredients to a shaker and dry-shake without ice. Add ice, reshake, and then strain into a chilled coupe. Garnish with the crystallized ginger.

Yellow Calico with Honeybees

CLAIRE FASHIONS A PLUG from gum arabic and a scrap of yellow calico printed with honeybees to close Captain Stebbings's wound in *An Echo in the Bone*. Bartenders, having different priorities, use the stuff to make gum syrup, which adds a silky texture, or mouthfeel, to spirit-heavy drinks. This one pairs rye whiskey, popular in the colonies, with Bénédictine for honeyed sweetness.

—⁓⁓⁓—

Style: 𝔐𝔬𝔡𝔢𝔯𝔫

—⁓⁓⁓—

2 ounces RYE WHISKEY

½ ounce BÉNÉDICTINE

½ ounce FRESHLY SQUEEZED LEMON JUICE

1 teaspoon GUM SYRUP
(page 191 or store-bought)

1 dash ANGOSTURA BITTERS

Add all the ingredients to a shaker half-filled with ice, shake to chill, and strain into a chilled cocktail glass.

The Governor's Personal Stores

W E KNOW FROM THE purser of the *Artemis* that Lord John Grey brought figs, sugar, and coffee with him for his voyage to Jamaica to be installed as governor. While he likely paired them with the Madeira wine he also stowed (a very nice combination) rather than the rougher sailor's rum on board, this drink uses rum for the eminent reason that it goes amazingly well with figs, coffee, and chocolate. Enjoy it with a rich dessert.

Style: 𝕸𝖔𝖉𝖊𝖗𝖓

2 ounces AGED BRITISH-STYLE RUM

½ ounce EAST INDIA SHERRY

½ ounce COLD BREW ESPRESSO

¼ ounce FIG SYRUP
(page 190)

2 or 3 dashes CHOCOLATE BITTERS

½ DRIED FIG for garnish

Stir all the ingredients in a mixing glass with plenty of ice and strain into a chilled rocks glass over a large cube of ice. Garnish with the fig.

Clearing the Brambles

THE THING ABOUT BRAMBLE bushes, as anybody who's grown them knows, is they tend to spread, pop up elsewhere, and generally take over if you don't keep cutting them back. Kind of like life's problems. Claire and Jamie have to work as hard to clear the land on Fraser's Ridge as they do to clear away the challenges that rise up in their family and community. This liquid metaphor comes from a riff by bartender Jeffrey Morgenthaler on a modern classic, the Bramble. Instead of the Bramble's base of gin, it's made with bourbon, more in keeping with the colonial Carolina setting. It's best with a bottled in bond or cask-strength bourbon.

Style: 𝔐𝔬𝔡𝔢𝔯𝔫

2 ounces BOURBON

½ ounce CRÈME DE MURE
(see note)

1 ounce FRESHLY SQUEEZED
LEMON JUICE

½ ounce SIMPLE SYRUP
(page 188)

1 dash ANGOSTURA BITTERS

1 slice of LEMON for garnish

Several FRESH BLACKBERRIES
for garnish

PEYCHAUD'S BITTERS
for garnish

Add all the ingredients to a cocktail shaker half-filled with ice, shake to chill, and strain into an Old-Fashioned glass filled with crushed ice. Garnish with the lemon slice, blackberries, and a dash or two of Peychaud's or other red-colored bitters on top.

NOTE: *If crème de mure is unavailable, substitute 1 teaspoon blackberry preserves and reduce the simple syrup to 1 barspoon.*

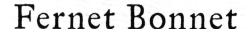

Fernet Bonnet

I T MAY SEEM ODD to reference one of *Outlander*'s most despicable villains, Stephen Bonnet, in a drink. There's almost nothing good in the man, yet his actions, like those of other villains, serve as a yardstick for other characters like Brianna to measure their capacity for empathy, even toward their enemies. Which brings us to Fernet Branca, one of the more feared and despised cocktail ingredients, with a taste that is sometimes described as "mouthwash served inside your grandfather's old leather shoe," or even worse. It's divisive. But as an ingredient in cocktails, it works magic like musk works in perfumes; it's the undertone, the hint of funk, the touch of evil that ties it all together. Tamed here with pirate's rum, coconut, and even an egg yolk in mimic of the colonial-era style of drinks known as flips, it may make you a fan of fernet. Or not.

Style: 𝕳𝖎𝖘𝖙𝖔𝖗𝖎𝖈𝖆𝖑

¾ ounce AGED JAMAICAN OR GUYANAN RUM (see note)

½ ounce FERNET BRANCA

¼ ounce BOURBON

½ ounce CINNAMON SYRUP (page 192)

1 ounce CREAM OF COCONUT

1 EGG YOLK

FRESHLY GRATED CINNAMON AND NUTMEG for garnish

Add all the ingredients to a shaker and dry-shake without ice. Add ice and reshake, strain into a chilled coupe, and garnish with freshly grated cinnamon and nutmeg.

NOTE: *A pot-distilled aged rum from Jamaica or Guyana or an aged overproof blended rum like Smith & Cross is the closest we can get to the rough eighteenth-century style of rum, so use one here.*

Murtagh's Oath

JAMIE'S GODFATHER, MURTAGH, personifies loyalty and trust. This cocktail takes its origin from the Godfather, an equal parts Scotch and amaretto liqueur cocktail from the 1970s named after another character with a somewhat different way of understanding loyalty. It ups the ratio of whisky to avoid the overly sweet taste of the original, splits the sweetener between amaretto and drier maraschino, and adds a few drops of bitters, as befits a man of few words.

Style: 𝔐𝔬𝔡𝔢𝔯𝔫

1½ ounces BLENDED SCOTCH

½ ounce ISLAY PEATED SINGLE MALT SCOTCH, preferably Lagavulin

½ ounce AMARETTO

½ ounce MARASCHINO LIQUEUR

1 dash ANGOSTURA BITTERS

1 dash ORANGE BITTERS

1 ORANGE PEEL for garnish

Add all the ingredients to a rocks glass with 1 large ice cube and stir to mix. Garnish with the orange peel.

Port Chocolate Wedding Cake

THERE IS NO EXTANT recipe for the delicious-looking wedding cake featured in season five's wedding between Brianna and Roger, and there is no mention of wedding cake in *The Fiery Cross*, though there is a feast of celebration, to be sure. Between the port-finished Scotch, the rum, brandy, and crème de cacao, this is definitely a "dessert in a glass" drink. Historians may point out that cutting the cake was not a wedding tradition in the colonial period, but a little liberty with history is surely forgivable with such a time-traveling couple.

—⁓⁓⁓—

Style: 𝔐𝔬𝔡𝔢𝔯𝔫

—⁓⁓⁓—

1½ ounces PORT-FINISHED SINGLE MALT SCOTCH

½ ounce APRICOT BRANDY

½ ounce AGED RUM

¼ ounce CRÈME DE CACAO

1 dash CHOCOLATE BITTERS

1 ORANGE PEEL for garnish

Stir all the ingredients in a mixing glass with plenty of ice, and strain into a chilled coupe. Garnish with the orange peel.

Walnut Nightcap

LIVING ON THE COLONIAL frontier meant making do with what you had, as when the Frasers made a meal from a green pumpkin that had been partially eaten by a rat. Jamie suggested it needed walnut ketchup—at that time "ketchup" meant any relish served with a meal—and he stated that the ketchup was made with anchovies and vinegar "and a few other things." This drink features a split base of rye whiskey and Scotch, and a few other things, including nocino, a liqueur made from green walnuts and spices. Better than walnut ketchup.

Style: 𝔐𝔬𝔡𝔢𝔯𝔫

1½ ounces RYE WHISKEY

½ ounce ISLAY PEATED SINGLE MALT SCOTCH

¼ ounce MARASCHINO LIQUEUR

¼ ounce NOCINO

2 dashes CACAO BITTERS

1 dash CARDAMOM TINCTURE (page 194)

1 slice APPLE or COOKED PUMPKIN WITH SKIN ON for garnish

Add all the ingredients to a mixing glass with ice and stir. Strain into a chilled rocks glass with fresh ice. Garnish with a slice of apple or, if available, a small slice of cooked pumpkin.

Sugar Plums
for Nessie

I N *AN ECHO IN THE BONE,* Lord John Grey visits Nessie the madam on Christmas Eve, bringing her a box of sugar plums, and the two share some information along with the sweets. There are a number of "Sugar Plum" cocktails online, but most seem to feature gin and grapefruit juice for some odd reason. In the eighteenth century, sugar plums actually referred to sugar-coated almonds or spice seeds and were called "plums" based on their size, not their ingredients. Neither seems to fit the poignancy of this scene between two characters whose lives necessitate keeping secrets. This recipe tries to stick closer to the historical sugar plums by infusing Scotch with fruits (which, as we know, has a long history) and adding nut and spice ingredients for a rich, sinful sipper. You can substitute another dry orange liqueur, but the brandy base in Grand Marnier really elevates this drink.

Style: 𝔜𝔦𝔰𝔱𝔬𝔯𝔦𝔠𝔞𝔩

2 ounces SUGAR PLUM WHISKY
(page 195)

½ ounce NOCINO

½ ounce GRAND MARNIER

¼ ounce AMARETTO

2 wide strips ORANGE PEEL,
1 for garnish

1 piece SUGAR PLUM
for garnish (optional)

Add all the ingredients, including 1 orange peel, to a shaker half-filled with ice and shake. Strain into a chilled coupe and garnish with the other orange peel and a piece of sugar plum, if available.

Granol Brose

A THOLL BROSE, THE TRADITIONAL Scottish dessert of oatmeal spiked with whisky, honey, and cream, is a verra fine thing. It was served at Lallybroch in *Outlander* and has graced many a table in Scotland up to the present day. But it is, admittedly, a bit one-dimensional, so how to do it differently, make it more modern? The answer is simple: make it with granola. The dried fruits and spices mimic the same ingredients often added to Atholl Brose, and the oil in the granola allows for fat-washing—the technique of infusing an oil or fat into whisky to create a thick, creamy mouthfeel. Make sure to taste the Scotch as it's infused with the granola so that it achieves the right flavor, and choose your granola well. You want to avoid artificial ingredients or too much added sugar.

Style: 𝕸𝖔𝖉𝖊𝖗𝖓

1½ cups ALL-NATURAL GRANOLA

1½ cups BLENDED SCOTCH WHISKY

¼ cup ROLLED OATS

¾ cup WATER

1½ cups HEAVY CREAM

2 tablespoons HONEY

GRANOLA, FRESH OR DRIED FRUITS, and/or WHIPPED CREAM for garnish

Add the granola and whisky to a glass container with a lid. Seal and store in a cool spot away from direct sunlight for at least 24 hours. Taste, and infuse for up to another day if needed. Strain through a fine-mesh strainer, discard the granola, and set the infused whisky aside. Stir the oats and water together in a bowl and let sit for several hours or overnight. Strain the liquid through cheesecloth and add the liquid to the infused whisky, along with the cream and honey. Refrigerate until chilled, then pour 4 ounces into a chilled mug or Old-Fashioned glass, and serve garnished with granola, fresh or dried fruits, and/or a tablespoon of whipped cream.

Duke of Suffolk

GIUSEPPE GONZÁLEZ IS FAMOUS in the bar industry for calling it as he sees it. So when he says this is his favorite drink creation (and he's created a couple of modern classics), believe him. This is basically a tea-based Irish coffee with gin instead of whiskey. The key is to pour the lightly whipped cream *slowly* on top of the gin-spiked tea to create an ethereal float that dissolves into the drink. Even Lord John Grey would be impressed.

Style: 𝕸𝖔𝖉𝖊𝖗𝖓

1½ ounces LONDON DRY GIN

4 or more ounces SWEET TEA
(see recipe at right)

1 tablespoon LIGHTLY WHIPPED
CREAM (see recipe at right)

Add the gin and sweet tea to a heatproof mug or teacup (extra points for using an antique teakettle and fancy cup and saucer). Slowly pour the cream down the side of the cup to float it on top.

Sweet Tea

Steep equal parts Earl Grey and English Breakfast teas. Sweeten the tea on a 3:1 ratio with ½ ounce simple syrup to each ½ cup of tea.

Lightly Whipped Cream

To make the lightly whipped cream, pour 1 tablespoon of heavy cream into a jar with a lid and shake until lightly whipped.

Strathspey Bracer

CLAIRE DANCES HER HEART OUT at an inn while on the road with Jamie early on in *Outlander*, despite admitting to a lack of dancing skill and feeling encumbered by eighteenth-century clothes and shoes. After she kicks off her clogs, she surprises herself and really gets into it until she's out of breath. It's one of the first scenes where she begins to enjoy life in the past. This cocktail featuring coffee would be a great restorative to Claire or anyone else tired out from dancing. If you don't have cream sherry, you can substitute a rich oloroso or Pedro Ximénez sherry.

Style: 𝕸𝖔𝖉𝖊𝖗𝖓

2 ounces AGED DARK RUM

1 ounce CREAM SHERRY

¾ ounce COLD BREW ESPRESSO

2 or 3 dashes CHOCOLATE BITTERS

½ DRIED FIG for garnish

Stir all the ingredients in a mixing glass with plenty of ice. Strain into a chilled rocks glass over a large ice cube and garnish with the fig.

Hot Spiced Daiquiri

YES, THE DAIQUIRI IS a quintessential warm-climate drink. But when the winter wind's blowing on the Ridge and the redcoats are coming, it's not so appealing. This adaptation of the revolutionary original cocktail by Kathleen Hawkins of Wright & Co. in Detroit (where they know about cold weather) may seem outlandish, but it *is* what you want to be drinking in winter. If you can't find Plantation pineapple rum, add 1 ounce pineapple juice and increase the aged rum by 1 ounce.

Style: 𝕸𝖔𝖉𝖊𝖗𝖓

4 ounces HOT WATER

1 ounce AGED RUM

1 ounce PLANTATION PINEAPPLE RUM

½ ounce CINNAMON SYRUP (page 192)

½ ounce FRESHLY SQUEEZED LIME JUICE

2 or 3 tablespoons ANGOSTURA WHIPPED CREAM (see recipe) for topping

FRESHLY GROUND CINNAMON for garnish

1 small CINNAMON STICK for garnish

Add all the ingredients to a heatproof mug, stir briefly to combine, and top with whipped cream. Garnish with a sprinkle of cinnamon and a cinnamon stick.

Angostura Whipped Cream

Whip 1 cup heavy cream with 16 dashes of Angostura bitters in a chilled metal bowl until stiff. Try it on your next dessert, too!

On the Table with the Quince Jelly

HERE'S ANOTHER SPICY ONE, referring to a chapter of *Dragonfly in Amber* in which Jamie is dragged along for a night of debauchery in Paris with assorted European nobles and their companions, then has to explain it all to an angry Claire. The name describes one of the locations where hanky-panky occurs at a house of prostitution, right between a saddle of mutton and boiled potatoes. Quinces, a relative of apples, have a long association with love and lust, with some myths naming it as the original apple that Paris gave to Aphrodite in return for Helen of Troy. (Look how that went!) Quince is really quite a delight when it has been cooked to soften it—it's too hard to eat raw. This recipe is a veritable love potion of vanilla and fruit flavors. And if no quinces are at hand, it works just as well with a firm, ripe pear.

Style: 𝕸𝖔𝖉𝖊𝖗𝖓

2 slices FRESH QUINCE or PEAR, 1 for garnish

1 tablespoon TURBINADO or Demerara sugar

2 ounces BOURBON

¼ ounce VANILLA SIMPLE SYRUP (page 191)

¼ teaspoon ORANGE BLOSSOM WATER

1 dash CARDAMOM TINCTURE (page 194)

3 dashes ORANGE BITTERS

If using quince, poach the slices for 5 minutes or more in boiling water until they begin to soften. Then caramelize the quince (or pear) slices by sprinkling them with sugar and running them under a broiler until golden brown and the sugar has begun to melt. Watch carefully to avoid burning them! Muddle 1 slice in a mixing glass, add all the other ingredients, and stir without ice. Add ice, stir to chill, and strain into a rocks glass with 1 large ice cube. Garnish with the other quince slice.

Chapter

FOUR

Sparkling
Beverages

CONTAINING Seven Recipes

To the Core

I F THE SEASON FOUR episode "The Deep Heart's Core" is about secrets and the harm that they can cause, the Yeats poem from which the title is taken is about finding peace and healing. This genever-and-calvados cocktail by Edinburgh bartender Iain McPherson employs two spirits that seem like they conflict but harmonize quite well. It may be just the thing to sip during serious conversations, sharing secrets, or enjoying a nontraumatic, quiet, peaceful moment.

Style: 𝕸𝖔𝖉𝖊𝖗𝖓

¾ ounce OLD DUFF GENEVER

½ ounce CALVADOS

¾ ounce FRESH APPLE JUICE

½ ounce SPARKLING ALCOHOLIC CIDER

⅓ ounce RICH SIMPLE SYRUP (page 188)

4 drops SALINE SOLUTION (1 part salt:10 parts water)

COLD SPARKLING WATER for topping

1 slice of APPLE for garnish

Build the ingredients in a Collins glass full of ice and top with sparkling water. Garnish with the apple slice.

Glasgow Mule

A MULE IN COCKTAIL TERMS is a long drink with ginger ale, after the OG mule, the vodka-based Moscow Mule. Naturally the Glasgow Mule, created by renowned bartender Damon Boelte, starts with Scotch but then adds fresh lemon, elderflower liqueur, and Angostura bitters to the mix. We hope Clarence would approve, even though he never went to Glasgow.

Style: 𝔐𝔬𝔡𝔢𝔯𝔫

1½ ounces BLENDED SCOTCH

½ ounce ELDERFLOWER LIQUEUR

¾ ounce FRESHLY SQUEEZED LEMON JUICE

1 dash ANGOSTURA BITTERS

4 ounces GINGER BEER

1 LEMON WHEEL for garnish

1 piece CANDIED GINGER for garnish

MINT SPRIGS for garnish

Pour all the ingredients into a Collins or copper mule glass, fill with crushed ice, and stir. Garnish with the lemon wheel and candied ginger skewered on a toothpick.

Father Fogden's Hacienda

WILD GUAVA TREES CLIMB up the walls of Father Fogden's house in *Voyager*. In some parts of the world, guavas do grow as invasive weeds, but in other areas, they are becoming more common as a fresh fruit in grocery stores. There are many recipes for guava cocktails, but most of them call for guava nectar, which often has added sugar and water. If you can find fresh or frozen guava, it will work much better in this drink; if not, a teaspoon of guava jelly would work better than nectar in this refreshing sparkling drink that can be appreciated by any visitors, shipwrecked or not. If guava juice is the last resort, use ¾ ounce.

Style: 𝕿𝖗𝖔𝖕𝖎𝖈𝖆𝖑

1 FRESH GUAVA, or ¼ of the extra-large South American guavas

2 ounces GOLD RUM

1 ounce FRESHLY SQUEEZED LIME JUICE

½ ounce ORANGE CURAÇAO or Triple Sec

SODA WATER for topping

1 slice GUAVA or LIME for garnish

If using fresh guava, muddle it in a cocktail shaker, and add all the other ingredients. Fill a mixing glass with crushed ice and shake to chill. Strain into a tall glass filled with fresh cracked ice and top off with soda water. Garnish with the slice of guava or lime, and keep away from dogs, sheep, and coconuts named Coco.

Holiday Clove Spritz

THIS RECIPE TAKES ITS cue from the traditional Christmas decoration of studding an orange with cloves. Although cloves would have been very hard to come by on Fraser's Ridge, some of the older inhabitants would surely have memories of these fragrant objects from their childhoods in Scotland. Turning this idea into a spritz with a clove-flavored liqueur from Barbados stays true to the Fraser family's Caribbean connection and makes for a light yet flavorful drink suitable for any holiday.

Style: 𝕸𝖔𝖉𝖊𝖗𝖓

2 ounces LONDON DRY GIN

1 ounce FRESHLY SQUEEZED LEMON JUICE

½ ounce VELVET FALERNUM

½ ounce APEROL

SODA WATER for topping

ORANGE PEEL studded with a clove or two for garnish

Add all the ingredients to a shaker half-filled with ice and shake. Strain into a tall glass filled with ice and top with soda water. Garnish with the clove-studded orange peel.

SPARKLING BEVERAGES

Storm's End Grog

SHIPWRECK, STORMS, AND SUSPENSE typify the last chapters of *Voyager*, which narrate a tragic confluence among Claire, Jamie, and their companions trying to avoid capture by the English; enslaved Africans trying to gain their freedom; and a British warship trying to stop both groups. This concoction blends Old World spirits typical of the British navy at that time with spice and coconut for taking one's ease on land or sea after rough weather. If available, use a navy-strength gin, which has a higher alcohol content.

Style: **Tropical**

1½ ounces LONDON DRY GIN

½ ounce KRONAN SWEDISH PUNSCH
(or substitute an
aged English-style rum)

¾ ounce FRESHLY SQUEEZED
LIME JUICE

1 ounce CREAM OF COCONUT

½ ounce VELVET FALERNUM

2 or 3 dashes ANGOSTURA BITTERS
for garnish

1 FRESH LIME LEAF
(if not available, use a lime wheel)
for garnish

Combine all the ingredients in a cocktail shaker with a scoop of crushed ice and shake until chilled. Pour into a Collins glass and fill with more crushed ice. Garnish by dashing the Angostura on top of the drink and by adding the lime leaf.

Witchcraft

C LAIRE FACES MULTIPLE ACCUSATIONS of witchcraft in *Outlander*, being nearly burned at the stake soon after traveling back to the eighteenth century for the first time. Absinthe also faced persecution at the turn of the twentieth century, with claims of causing hallucinations, criminal violence, and madness. These claims caused it to be banned in much of Europe and the United States until the early twenty-first century. Thankfully, it can now be enjoyed without threat of prosecution in the form of this classic whisky cocktail from Jack Jamieson, where the only burning comes from the peated whisky.

Style: 𝔐𝔬𝔡𝔢𝔯𝔫

2 ounces ISLAY PEATED SINGLE
MALT SCOTCH WHISKY,
such as Laphroaig

½ ounce DRY CURAÇAO

½ ounce ABSINTHE

⅓ ounce RICH HONEY SYRUP
(page 192)

Juice of ½ LIME

SODA WATER for topping

FRESH MINT LEAF for garnish

Add all the ingredients to a highball glass filled with crushed ice. Swizzle to integrate and top with soda water. Garnish with the mint.

Shocking Orange Jell-O Shots

WHAT COULD BE LESS serious than the Jell-O shot, that staple of college parties and, dare we say, TV series watch parties? Although molecular mixologists and some high-end dessert chefs have tried to dress it up, it remains a simple guilty pleasure. Aperol adds orange candy flavor and color to rosé sparkling wine, and brandy punches up the alcohol content. (No need to use fancy brandy here.) Down these shots when you see the characters kiss, or hook up, or tell a lie, or whatever excuse you need to enjoy them. This recipe makes 12 shots or 6 coupe-size shots.

Style: 𝕸𝖔𝖉𝖊𝖗𝖓

6 ounces SPARKLING ROSÉ
or ROSÉ CHAMPAGNE

4 tablespoons POWDERED GELATIN

2 ounces APEROL

4 ounces BRANDY or COGNAC

2 ounces FRESHLY SQUEEZED
LEMON JUICE

2 ounces SIMPLE SYRUP
(page 188)

CITRUS TWISTS,
WHITE CHOCOLATE FLAKES,
COLORED SPRINKLES,
or EDIBLE FLOWERS for garnish

Slowly heat the sparkling wine in a small saucepan, add the gelatin, and stir to dissolve. Remove from the heat and allow to cool. Add the Aperol, brandy, lemon juice, and simple syrup. Stir to mix, pour into 12 shot glasses or 6 coupe glasses, and chill overnight. Garnish each with a citrus twist, white chocolate flakes, sprinkles, and/or flowers.

Chapter

FIVE

Wine, Beer, and Cider Drinks

CONTAINING Seven Recipes

Appellation Cooler

WHAT'S IN A NAME? The baby boy born to Rachel and Young Ian in *Written in My Own Heart's Blood* goes by Oggy, short for Oglethorpe, after the founder of the province of Georgia. It isn't until *Go Tell the Bees That I Am Gone* that he is given a new name by Ian's former wife from his time in the Mohawk nation—Wakyo'teyehsnonhsa, who was nicknamed Emily. The fact that Ian and Emily were unable to have a child together makes the scene quite touching, and most will agree that Hunter is a better name than Oglethorpe. Which brings us to the Appellation Cooler (appellation means "the act of naming") by renowned bartender Natasha David. It's a terrific low-alcohol option for baptisms, baby-naming ceremonies, or just brunch. This recipe can easily be scaled up to pitcher size when serving many guests.

Style: 𝕸𝖔𝖉𝖊𝖗𝖓

2 ounces DRY WHITE WINE

1 ounce COCCHI AMERICANO

1 ounce BASIL-INFUSED BIANCO VERMOUTH (see recipe at right)

1 teaspoon APRICOT LIQUEUR

2 ounces DRY SPARKLING WINE

1 slice CUCUMBER for garnish

In a large wine glass, combine all the ingredients over ice. Stir to chill and incorporate. Generously garnish with the cucumber slice.

To make basil-infused bianco vermouth, add 20 fresh basil leaves to a 750ml bottle of Dolin blanc vermouth. Let steep for 24 hours, strain, and refrigerate until ready to use. This recipe can be cut in half or quartered to make smaller amounts.

Redbrick Wall

STONE FENCE OR STONEWALL was the name of a common colonial drink of hard cider and rum, both products of New England and doubtless a reference to the area's ubiquitous stone walls—or maybe it was a reference to the effect on one's skull after a night of overindulgence. Colonial North Carolina was built with bricks made from the local red clay, and it was not a center of either rum or cider production. However, its location between the Caribbean and the northeastern states ensured that both beverages were plentiful and cheap, and historical records indicate the inhabitants were mighty fond of both. This mix is ideal for sitting on or leaning up against a garden wall on a sunny day.

Style: 𝕳𝖎𝖘𝖙𝖔𝖗𝖎𝖈

1½ ounces AGED POT-STILL RUM

½ ounce FRESHLY SQUEEZED LEMON JUICE

½ ounce FRESHLY SQUEEZED ORANGE JUICE

2 ounces DRY SPARKLING CIDER for topping (see note)

2 dashes ANGOSTURA BITTERS for garnish

Add all the ingredients to a chilled tall glass or mug filled with ice, stir briefly to combine, and top with the cider. Dash the Angostura bitters on top.

NOTE: *Made with hard cider, this is a potent but drier and more savory drink. Made with nonalcoholic cider, it will be sweeter but more sessionable.*

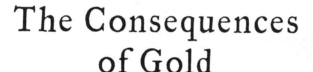

The Consequences of Gold

WHAT'S A ROMANCE WITHOUT hidden treasure? There's the "Frenchman's gold," the historical gold coins—known as *Louis d'or*—donated mostly not by any Frenchman but by Spain to the Jacobite cause, some of which were never accounted for and gave rise to all sorts of actual historical treasure hunts. There's the portion of that treasure that in *Outlander* is smuggled to North Carolina by Jocasta and her husband, Hector. And there's Geillis Duncan's money that she pilfered from her husband, also to back the Scottish rebellion, that she later uses for her own nefarious schemes as well. This simple golden drink is guilt-free and combines a fortified wine from the Gascony region of France, a Spanish liqueur flavored with forty-three ingredients, and a bitter gentian liqueur to remind us that stolen treasure often comes with harsh consequences.

— ✕✕✕✕✕✕ —

Style: 𝕸𝖔𝖉𝖊𝖗𝖓

— ✕✕✕✕✕✕ —

1½ ounces PINEAU DES CHARENTES BLANC

¾ ounce CUARENTA Y TRES or YELLOW CHARTREUSE

¾ ounce SUZE or other French gentian liqueur (see note)

EDIBLE YELLOW FLOWER PETALS or edible gold leaf flakes for garnish

Add all the ingredients to a mixing glass and stir; strain into a chilled coupe. Garnish with a few golden flower petals or, if you're feeling rich, a few flakes of edible gold leaf.

NOTE: *Try playing around with the ratios of the liqueurs to suit your taste for more or less spice or bitterness.*

Stout and Full Hearts

TOASTS ARE FOR CONGRATULATIONS, for commemorations, for rekindling the bonds of love, friendship, and loyalty, whether pledged in whisky, beer, or, in this case, both. Adding distilled spirits to beer or ale is one of the oldest mixological moves, and while stout beer is usually associated with Ireland, Scottish brewers have been making similar stuff for centuries. In fact, some have called Scottish sweet stout the country's most distinctive type of beer. This beer-based cocktail makes for a fine, foamy toast, and if the banana liqueur is totally ahistorical, it belongs here because it works so well with the other ingredients. If you can't find a Scottish stout, substitute another style of stout, but don't tell anyone. *Slàinte!*

Style: **Historical**

1½ ounces BLENDED SCOTCH

½ ounce BANANA LIQUEUR

1 ounce CHILLED ESPRESSO

2 dashes CHOCOLATE BITTERS

SCOTTISH STOUT for topping

Add all the ingredients except the stout to a mixing glass half-filled with ice and stir. Strain into a chilled mug and top with stout to your taste.

Peaches in a Boot

"SEAMEN WILL DRINK *ANYTHING*," the purser of the *Porpoise* tells Claire, even "peaches mashed inside a rubber boot and left to ferment." Unsurprisingly, this Peaches in a Boot drink is much better, since it requires no fermentation time and delivers light, summery flavors. The Cognac and peaty Scotch give it depth and a touch of fermented funk—without the boot.

Style: 𝔐𝔬𝔡𝔢𝔯𝔫

2 PEACH WEDGES, 1 for garnish

2 ounces ROSÉ WINE

½ ounce COGNAC

1 teaspoon LAPHROAIG 10-YEAR SCOTCH

¾ ounce PEACH LIQUEUR

¾ ounce FRESHLY SQUEEZED LEMON JUICE

¼ ounce SIMPLE SYRUP (page 188)

In a shaker, muddle 1 peach wedge. Add all the other ingredients and shake with ice, then double-strain into a chilled coupe. Garnish with the remaining peach wedge.

Something Winked Red

T HE LAST FEW PAGES of *Drums of Autumn* see the Highland families attending a Gathering at Mount Helicon, and Roger and Bree finally agree to marry. As he takes her hand, the firelight shines on a ruby ring, which Jamie had once placed on Claire's finger (though it was too large) when they were married. This concoction, redolent of summer and fall fruit flavors, will not come out ruby red, but it will be red enough to speak of enduring love.

Style: **Modern**

¾ ounce PEAR BRANDY

2 ounces BIANCO VERMOUTH

1 teaspoon RASPBERRY SYRUP
(page 191)

½ ounce FRESHLY SQUEEZED
LEMON JUICE

1 barspoon SEVILLE ORANGE
MARMALADE

ROSÉ CHAMPAGNE
or SPARKLING ROSÉ
for topping

2 or 3 RASPBERRIES for garnish

Add all the ingredients to a shaker half-filled with ice and shake to chill. Strain into a wine glass or champagne flute and top with rosé Champagne or sparkling wine. Garnish with the fresh raspberries.

Jenny's Flip

J AMIE SUGGESTS THAT JENNY should drink ale with raw eggs after she gives birth to Ian early in *Voyager*. Although flips, or drinks with a whole egg beaten into them, were popular in colonial times, it's rare to find one on a modern bar's drink list (and even Jenny demanded whisky instead). Egg whites are much more common and lend frothiness to sours and other drinks. A whole egg, however, gives an even thicker, creamier texture. If drinking an egg sounds odd, remember that many milkshake recipes include an egg, and the rum, spice, and molasses are a persuasive if not restorative mix.

— ⁓⁓⁓⁓ —

Style: 𝕳𝖎𝖘𝖙𝖔𝖗𝖎𝖈

— ⁓⁓⁓⁓ —

6 ounces BROWN ALE

2 ounces DARK RUM

1 ounce DARK MOLASSES

½ ounce BÉNÉDICTINE

½ ounce HEAVY CREAM

1 EGG

FRESHLY GRATED NUTMEG and CINNAMON for garnish

Heat the ale in a saucepan until hot but not boiling. Add all the other ingredients to a heatproof mixing bowl and stir or whisk until frothy. Slowly add the hot ale to the bowl while stirring constantly. Pour into a heatproof mug and garnish with freshly grated nutmeg and cinnamon.

Chapter

SIX

—⁓—

Non-Alcoholic Beverages

CONTAINING Five Recipes

Dr. Stern's Prescription

THE FRENCH 75 is a classic gin cocktail topped with Champagne that has spawned dozens of variations. This one is alcohol-free, using ginger and pineapple, ingredients common to eighteenth-century Hispaniola—modern-day Haiti and the Dominican Republic. It's a useful thirst-quencher when you need to stay sharp for botanizing or other outdoor activities.

Style: 𝕬lcohol=free

¼ cup FRESH PINEAPPLE, diced

¾ ounce GINGER HONEY SYRUP (page 190)

¾ ounce FRESHLY SQUEEZED LIME JUICE

CLUB SODA or SPARKLING WATER for topping

1 thin slice FRESH GINGER,
½ slice LIME,
1 slice PINEAPPLE with rind on,
and/or 1 pineapple leaf
for garnish (see note)

Muddle the fresh pineapple in a tall glass. Add all the other ingredients and stir to combine. Fill the glass with ice and top off with club soda. Lay the slice of ginger on top and garnish with the other items.

NOTE: *Tropical-style drinks often go big with garnishes, and nonalcoholic drinks benefit from the extra fragrance and visual appeal, so don't skimp on them here!*

Consolation Cup

MINT TEA HAS PROVIDED comfort along with sprightly flavor for millennia. It's part of Claire's herbal remedies and is mixed in the poppy syrup she gives to ease Alex Randall's terminal suffering. This happier brew needs no drugs to lift the spirits, instead relying on orange blossom water to accentuate the wild, grassy flavor of green tea. It is easily scaled up to provide a summer punch with the addition of sparkling water and fresh sliced fruits.

Style: 𝕬𝖑𝖈𝖔𝖍𝖔𝖑-𝖋𝖗𝖊𝖊

4 ounces FRESH BREWED GREEN TEA

2 ounces FRESH BREWED MINT TEA

¼ ounce SIMPLE SYRUP
(page 188)

A few drops ORANGE BLOSSOM
WATER

Sprig of FRESH MINT and/or FRESH
ORANGE BLOSSOM for garnish

Brew the green tea and spearmint separately, as green tea needs a lower water temperature and different time to steep, depending on the type. Spearmint, like most herbal teas, needs boiling water. Let cool and combine in a ratio of 2:1. Stir in the simple syrup and sprinkle a few drops of orange blossom water on top, but be sparing because orange blossom water can easily overpower other flavors. Add ice and garnish with the sprig of fresh mint and/or fresh orange blossom.

Almond Squirt

ALL THE FLAVORS THAT make tropical drinks so refreshing—like coconut, passion fruit, orgeat, and citrus—work just as well without alcohol. Almond squirts are traditional Scottish cookies made from ground almonds and egg whites; they were served at Lallybroch during the Hogmanay (New Year) celebrations. This liquid "squirt" uses coconut cream rather than eggs and works as a festive treat at New Year's or any other celebration.

Style: 𝕬𝖑𝖈𝖔𝖍𝖔𝖑-𝖋𝖗𝖊𝖊

2 ounces CREAM OF COCONUT

1 ounce FRESH or FROZEN PASSION FRUIT PULP

½ ounce ORGEAT SYRUP

½ ounce FRESHLY SQUEEZED LEMON JUICE

½ ounce FRESHLY SQUEEZED LIME JUICE

SODA WATER for topping

½ PASSION FRUIT SHELL and/or 1 LIME WHEEL for garnish

Add all the ingredients to a shaker half-filled with ice and shake well. Strain into a tall glass filled with crushed ice, and top with soda water. Garnish with half a passion fruit shell, if available, and/or a lime wheel. Consider upping your garnish game by adding shaved dark chocolate, edible flower petals, or a bit of lime zest on top!

Sneaky Fergus

IF HE WASN'T SO adorable, he'd be even more trouble. Fergus Fraser, born an orphan in Paris named Claudel, won over more than a few hearts in the books and series due to a combination of impishness, loyalty to Jamie, and a talent for getting on regardless of laws or morality. Riffing on a Scotch whisky punch recipe titled Sneaky Peat by Birmingham, Alabama, bartender Laura Newman, this recipe removes the alcohol to maintain innocence among old and young alike and gets its smoky flavor from Lapsang Souchong tea.

Style: **Alcohol-free**

1 cup CHILLED EXTRA-STRONG OOLONG TEA

2 cups CHILLED EXTRA-STRONG LAPSANG SOUCHONG TEA

2½ tablespoons SPICED SIMPLE SYRUP (page 192)

1 cup plus 2 tablespoons CHILLED CRANBERRY SYRUP (page 190)

½ cup WATER

¾ cup FRESHLY SQUEEZED LEMON JUICE

FRESH or DRIED CRANBERRIES and/or LEMON SLICES for garnish

Steep both teas separately using 1½ tablespoons loose tea or 3 tea bags for each cup of water and allow to cool. Add the teas to all the other ingredients in a pitcher and stir. Pour into ice-filled glasses and garnish with cranberries and/or lemon slices.

Garden of Fertility

I F YOU ONLY KNOW grenadine from an artificially colored bottle in the supermarket, you're in for a treat. Homemade grenadine made from pomegranate juice has more depth of flavor and is far more wholesome since you have more control over how much sugar is added. It's surprising the pomegranate doesn't make much of an appearance in *Outlander,* given its ancient symbolism connecting it to death but also to fertility and childbirth and its use in herbal medicine. Fun fact: Author Diana Gabaldon herself grows pomegranates in her garden! Combined with lime, cinnamon, and ginger ale or beer, pomegranates are good in all seasons as a stomach soother or just to recover from the toils of daily life.

Style: 𝕬𝖑𝖈𝖔𝖍𝖔𝖑-𝖋𝖗𝖊𝖊

2 ounces HOMEMADE GRENADINE
(page 193)

½ ounce CINNAMON SYRUP
(page 192)

¾ ounce FRESHLY SQUEEZED
LIME JUICE

GINGER ALE or BEER for topping

1 LIME WHEEL and/or FRESH
POMEGRANATE SEEDS for garnish

Add all the ingredients to a tall glass filled with ice and stir to mix. Top with ginger ale or beer and garnish with the lime wheel and/or fresh pomegranate seeds.

Chapter

SEVEN

Syrups, Tinctures, and Mixers

CONTAINING *Eighteen Recipes*

SYRUPS

Simple syrup, made from equal parts sugar and water, is a cocktail essential for adding not only sweetness but also viscosity, creating what's known as a thicker mouthfeel. Rich simple syrup, using double the amount of sugar to water, is even better at thickening, though it's also sweeter. Flavored simple syrups are an easy way of adding flavor quickly without having to grate fresh spices or juice fruits on the spot. Avoid making large amounts unless you're going to use it all quickly; simple syrups begin to lose flavor after a couple of weeks in the refrigerator and will eventually turn rancid. However, adding a tablespoon of high-proof vodka or light rum per cup of syrup will extend the refrigerated shelf life for at least a month or two.

Birch Water Syrup

Makes *about ¾ cup*

4 ounces BIRCH WATER (see note)

¾ cup SUGAR

Combine the birch water and sugar in a saucepan and heat gently until the sugar is dissolved. Cool, pour into a glass jar, and refrigerate if not using right away.

NOTE: *Birch water or birch syrup can be found in some natural and health food stores; if unavailable, substitute an equal amount of flat birch beer soda or, if all else fails, use coconut water.*

Black Pepper Honey Syrup

Makes *about 1 cup*

6 ounces HONEY

3 ounces WATER

1 tablespoon CRACKED BLACK PEPPERCORNS

Combine all the ingredients in a saucepan and simmer for 20 minutes. Cool and strain into a glass jar. Refrigerate until ready to use.

Cranberry Syrup

Makes *about 1½ cups*

1 cup WATER

1 cup SUGAR

1 cup FRESH or FROZEN CRANBERRIES
(see note)

Combine all the ingredients in a saucepan and bring to a boil. Lower the heat and simmer for 3 or 4 minutes or until fragrant. Remove from the heat, roughly mash the berries with a potato masher or spoon, and allow to cool. Strain into a glass jar and refrigerate if not using immediately.

NOTE: *Cranberry pairs easily with many other flavors so, depending on the recipe you're using it in, feel free to make variations: add a few strips of citrus rind, a stick of cinnamon and/or a couple of cloves, or a sprig of rosemary or other herb.*

Fig Syrup

Makes *about 1 cup*

1½ cups sliced DRIED FIGS

1 cup WATER

¾ cup RAW SUGAR

1 dash VANILLA EXTRACT

1 teaspoon FRESHLY SQUEEZED
LEMON JUICE

Combine all the ingredients in a small saucepan and simmer for 15 minutes over low heat. Let the syrup cool for about an hour to steep, then strain into a glass jar and refrigerate until using.

Ginger Honey Syrup

Makes *about 1¾ cups*

1 cup HONEY

One 6-inch knob of GINGER,
peeled and sliced

1 cup WATER

Combine all the ingredients in a saucepan and bring just to a boil. Reduce the heat and simmer for 5 minutes. Let cool and then refrigerate overnight. Strain into a glass jar to remove the solids and store in the refrigerator.

Gum Syrup

Makes *about ¾ cup*

¾ cup WATER

4 tablespoons POWDERED GUM ARABIC

1⅓ cups SUGAR

Heat ¼ cup of the water until nearly boiling, pour over the gum arabic in a glass jar, and stir to combine. Let sit for a couple of hours and stir again. Heat the remaining ½ cup water and the sugar until dissolved, and slowly add the gum arabic mixture. Simmer for 5 minutes while stirring. Let cool and skim off any foam or lumps that remain on top. Bottle and refrigerate. It will keep for at least 1 month.

Raspberry Syrup

Makes *about 4 ounces*

4 ounces RASPBERRIES

4 ounces SUGAR

Add the raspberries and sugar to a bowl and mash them together. Seal and refrigerate for a few days, stirring occasionally. Strain out the syrup that forms, bottle it, and refrigerate if not using immediately.

Lavender Honey Syrup

Makes *about 1 cup*

½ cup HONEY

½ cup WATER

1 tablespoon FRESH or DRIED LAVENDER LEAVES

Combine the honey with the water in a saucepan and heat until dissolved. Add the lavender leaves and let sit for 1 hour. Stir to combine and taste every 15 minutes; strain into a glass jar when the desired flavor profile is achieved. Let cool and refrigerate if not using right away.

Vanilla Simple Syrup

Makes *about 1¼ cups*

1 cup WATER

1 cup SUGAR

1 VANILLA BEAN, split lengthwise

Combine the water and sugar in a small saucepan over medium heat and stir until the sugar is completely dissolved. Remove from the heat and add the vanilla bean. Let steep for several hours. Strain into a glass jar or bottle, seal, and keep refrigerated.

Rich Honey Syrup

Makes *about 1 cup*

¾ cup HONEY

¼ cup HOT WATER

Combine the honey with the hot water in a glass jar and stir. Let cool. If not using immediately, store in the refrigerator, then warm before using. A neutral wildflower honey works best, but you can experiment with other honey varieties such as orange blossom.

Spiced Simple Syrup

Makes *about 1¼ cups*

1 cup SUGAR

1 cup WATER

1 STAR ANISE POD

½ teaspoon FRESHLY GROUND ALLSPICE

4 or 5 WHOLE CLOVES

1 teaspoon FRESHLY GRATED NUTMEG

¼ teaspoon FRESHLY GROUND CINNAMON

Combine all the ingredients in a saucepan and heat until the sugar dissolves completely. Let cool and strain through a paper coffee filter into a glass jar. Refrigerate if not using immediately.

Strawberry Basil Syrup

Makes *about 1½ cups*

1 cup sliced FRESH STRAWBERRIES

1 cup SUGAR

1 cup WATER

10 to 12 FRESH BASIL LEAVES

Combine the strawberries, sugar, and water and bring to a boil in a saucepan. Remove from the heat, add the basil leaves, and let cool for 1 hour. Strain into a glass jar, pressing the berries lightly to release their juice, and refrigerate if not using immediately. Different strains of basil (purple, Thai, lemon) will add different colors and flavors; try some out if you can find them!

Cinnamon Syrup

Makes *about 2 cups*

1 cup SUGAR

1 cup WATER

3 CINNAMON STICKS, broken into small pieces

Combine the sugar and water in a small saucepan over medium heat and stir until the sugar has dissolved. Remove from the heat, add the cinnamon pieces, and stir to combine. Cover and infuse for at least 6 hours. Strain through a paper coffee filter into a glass jar or bottle. It will keep, tightly sealed and refrigerated, for up to 1 month.

TINCTURES AND MIXERS

Tinctures are the bartender's spice cabinet, used in dashes to add pure flavor, just as vanilla and almond extracts—which are also tinctures—are used in cooking and baking. The basic recipe for the Cardamom Tincture on the next page can be used for most spices. Whole spices like cinnamon sticks or bay leaves should be broken into pieces or cracked in a mortar and pestle, and in general whole or freshly ground spices are preferred.

Homemade Grenadine

Makes *about 2½ cups*

2 large POMEGRANATES
(or 2 cups unsweetened pomegranate juice)

2 cups SUGAR

2 ounces POMEGRANATE MOLASSES

1 teaspoon ORANGE BLOSSOM WATER

1 ounce HIGH-PROOF VODKA
(optional)

Cut the pomegranates in half and juice using a citrus press. (This should yield about 2 cups of juice.) Pour the juice into a large glass measuring cup or other microwave-safe container and microwave at full power for 1 to 2 minutes, until warm. Add the sugar and stir until it dissolves completely. Add the pomegranate molasses and orange blossom water and stir to combine. Allow to cool, then bottle. Add the vodka as a preservative, if using.

Cardamom Tincture

Makes *1 cup*

¼ cup WHOLE GREEN CARDAMOM PODS,
lightly crushed in a mortar and pestle

4 ounces EVERCLEAR or
HIGH-PROOF VODKA

4 ounces WATER

Add the cardamom to the Everclear in a glass
jar and infuse for 3 days. Strain through a paper
coffee filter into a glass jar and add the water. It
will keep indefinitely.

Barley Water

Makes *about 3 cups*

*This recipe goes lighter on the lemon juice than is
typical because it is paired with lemon juice in the
cocktail recipes in this book. If serving on its own,
double the amount of lemon juice.*

¼ cup PEARL BARLEY

3 cups WATER

1 teaspoon SUGAR

1 tablespoon FRESHLY SQUEEZED
LEMON JUICE

Sort through the barley to remove any tiny stones
or debris. Rinse several times in water and drain
thoroughly, rubbing the grains and removing
any husks or broken grains that rise to the top
of the water. Soak the grains overnight or for at
least 6 hours. Drain, add to a pot with the 3 cups
water, the sugar, and the lemon juice, and bring
to a boil. Reduce the heat, cover, and simmer for
40 to 50 minutes, or until the barley is soft and
mushy (an Instant Pot or pressure cooker will
reduce this cooking time). Strain into a glass jar
and refrigerate until ready to use.

Toasted Coconut Tincture

𝕸𝖆𝖐𝖊𝖘 *about 4 ounces*

This is a variation on the Coconut Blast #3, invented at The Rockwell Place in Brooklyn, that can be used to add a hit of coconut flavor to any drink but particularly those made with brown spirits.

¼ cup UNSWEETENED COCONUT FLAKES

⅔ cup ORGANIC UNREFINED COCONUT OIL

3¾ ounces EVERCLEAR (190 proof)

1⅓ ounces WATER

Toast the coconut flakes in a heated skillet until light brown and fragrant. Watch closely and stir frequently to avoid burning. Heat the coconut oil in a double boiler until it becomes transparent, then add the oil and flakes to the Everclear in a wide-mouthed jar, seal it, and allow it to infuse for at least 5 hours, shaking occasionally. When the desired flavor is reached, place the infusion in the freezer overnight. Remove and discard the solidified fat, and strain the infusion through a paper coffee filter into another wide-mouthed jar. If necessary, filter again with a fresh filter. Add the water. It will keep indefinitely.

Sugar Plum Whisky

𝕸𝖆𝖐𝖊𝖘 *750ml*

750ml bottle of UNPEATED SINGLE MALT SCOTCH WHISKY

¼ cup DRIED FRUITS (raisins, currants, chopped dates in any combination)

2 DRIED FIGS

2 DRIED APRICOTS

2 DRIED PRUNES

1 long strip of TANGERINE PEEL or ORANGE PEEL

1 CINNAMON STICK

1 STAR ANISE POD

To the bottle of whisky, add the dried fruits, figs, apricots, prunes, citrus peel, cinnamon stick, and star anise. Infuse in a cool, dark place for 1 day. Taste, and continue to infuse for up to 3 days, tasting daily until the desired flavor is achieved. Strain through a fine strainer and strain again through a coffee filter, then rebottle. Store in a cool, dark location to preserve the flavor. It will keep indefinitely.

Chapter

EIGHT

—

Bar Bites
and
Appetizers

CONTAINING *Fifteen Recipes*

Fergus's Potatoes

WITH
CAVIAR

— ✺ —

Makes *20 to 30 potato bites*

— ✺ —

8 ounces BABY GOLD, fingerling, or peewee POTATOES

1 tablespoon KOSHER SALT

¾ teaspoon FLAKY SEA SALT, such as Maldon

6 tablespoons CRÈME FRAÎCHE

1 ounce STURGEON or PADDLEFISH CAVIAR

FRESH CHIVES, cut into ¾-inch lengths, for serving

CLAIRE MAY HAVE taught the Scots how to plant and harvest potatoes, but Fergus knew how to enjoy them: "You eat them with salt. Butter's good, if you have it" ("Field of Dreams," *Dragonfly in Amber*). Instead of what was likely tangy, cultured butter, this recipe uses crème fraîche (sour cream will work in a pinch) and takes these elegant bites a step further, topping them with a scoop of briny caviar. If you can't find sturgeon or paddlefish caviar, trout or salmon roe is also delicious here, and even flaked smoked mackerel will work. Use the smallest Yukon golds or fingerlings you can find, noting that you may have to increase the simmering time by a few minutes for potatoes that are on the larger side. The potatoes are best eaten at room temperature or slightly warm with the cold crème fraîche dolloped on right before serving. And while still delicious without the chives, they're worth including for the brightness they bring to the dish, for both palate and eyes. These celebratory hors d'oeuvres demand something equally decadent to sip on; make the Lavender Sachet on page 55 with your favorite Champagne.

———————— ✦ ————————

1. In a large saucepan, combine the potatoes with enough cold water to cover by 1 inch. Add the kosher salt, cover, and bring to a boil over high heat. Uncover, reduce the heat to medium, and simmer until a paring knife inserted into the center of a potato slides out with little resistance, 10 to 20 minutes, depending on the size of your potatoes. Drain and let cool for at least 20 minutes.

2. Halve the potatoes, arrange on a platter or tray, cut side up, and sprinkle evenly with the flaky salt. Stir the crème fraîche to loosen, then use a spoon to dollop a scant teaspoon onto the center of each potato half. Top with the caviar, dividing evenly among the potatoes. Place 1 to 2 chive pieces on top of each potato and serve.

Deviled "SCOTCH" Eggs

Makes 12 deviled eggs

6 large EGGS,
at room temperature

1 tablespoon UNSALTED
BUTTER

¼ cup UNSEASONED PANKO
BREAD CRUMBS

¾ teaspoon FENNEL SEEDS,
lightly crushed

½ teaspoon FRESHLY GROUND
BLACK PEPPER

½ teaspoon DRIED RUBBED SAGE

¼ teaspoon GARLIC POWDER

⅛ teaspoon KOSHER SALT

PINCH OF CAYENNE (optional)

¼ cup MAYONNAISE

1 tablespoon WHOLE-GRAIN
MUSTARD

1 teaspoon WHITE WINE
VINEGAR

¼ teaspoon WORCESTERSHIRE
SAUCE

DEVILED EGGS ARE a no-brainer for a versatile cocktail party snack. This version draws inspiration from traditional Scotch eggs, eschewing the ungainly size and laborious deep-frying. Crunchy panko bread crumbs mimic the texture of the breaded, fried eggs, and added fennel and sage are an ode to the classic flavors of breakfast sausage. Use a mortar and pestle or the bottom of a skillet to crush the fennel seeds; you want the texture to be coarse but with no whole seeds remaining. Though fresh herbs are usually preferred, dried rubbed sage (sometimes just labeled "dried sage" or "ground sage") works best here. Feel free to substitute distilled white vinegar for the white wine vinegar if that's what you have on hand. Play off the licorice-y fennel seed when choosing a cocktail pairing and swizzle up the Witchcraft on page 156, which features absinthe.

1. In a large saucepan, combine the eggs with enough cold water to cover by 1 inch. Bring to a boil over medium-high heat, then immediately remove the pan from the heat, cover, and let sit for 10 minutes. Meanwhile, combine 6 cups of cold water and 4 cups of ice in a bowl. Use a slotted spoon to transfer the eggs directly to the ice bath and let sit for at least 10 minutes.

2. While the eggs cool, melt the butter in an 8-inch skillet over medium-low heat. Add the panko and fennel seeds and cook, stirring and shaking the pan often, until fragrant and the crumbs are evenly browned, 2 to 4 minutes. Remove the pan from the heat and stir in the pepper, sage, garlic powder, salt, and cayenne (if using). Transfer to a bowl and let cool completely.

3. Peel the eggs and halve lengthwise. Scoop out the yolks and add to the bowl of a food processor along with the mayonnaise, mustard, vinegar, and Worcestershire. Process until smooth, about 1 minute, scraping down the sides of the bowl as needed. Transfer the filling to a piping bag fitted with a star tip and pipe into the egg white halves. Transfer to a serving platter, sprinkle with the panko mixture, and serve.

Bree's Pigs in a Blanket

—⌁—

Makes *18 pigs*

—⌁—

1 EGG, lightly beaten

2 tablespoons DIJON MUSTARD

2 teaspoons WATER

1 (14-ounce) package FROZEN PUFF PASTRY, thawed

6 HOT DOGS, cut into thirds crosswise

SESAME and/or POPPY SEEDS for sprinkling (optional)

I N "BOTTOM OF THE NINTH" (*Drums of Autumn*), Bree reminisces about drinking beer and eating hot dogs at a baseball game. While we have nothing against a ballpark frank, these top-drawer pigs in a blanket are everything good about that nostalgic treat distilled into a flaky, tangy, bite-size package. Our favorite puff pastry is the all-butter version from Dufour, which you can find in the freezer section of grocery stores alongside the pie crusts. Choose high-quality, all-beef frankfurters here. While 2 tablespoons may seem like a lot of Dijon mustard, the sharpness is welcome alongside the rich pastry and meat. For a second hit of mustard, you can serve these with your favorite spicy brown, German, or even good old yellow version for dipping and, while optional, Bree would want you to drink a beer. (Or at least a beer-based cocktail like the Stout and Full Hearts on page 169.)

———◆———

1. Heat the oven to 400°F. Line a rimmed baking sheet with parchment paper. In a small bowl, beat the egg with the mustard and water until homogeneous.

2. On a lightly floured counter, roll the pastry into a 12 by 15-inch rectangle. Use a pizza wheel or sharp knife to slice the rectangle lengthwise into six 2-inch strips. Working with one strip at a time, brush the top liberally with the egg wash, then cut into thirds crosswise. Place 1 hot dog piece across the short end of each rectangle, roll up, and place seam side down on the prepared baking sheet. Repeat with the remaining pastry strips and hot dogs; reserve the remaining egg wash. Refrigerate the pigs until firm, at least 20 minutes or up to 1 day.

3. Brush the tops of the rolls with egg wash (you may not use it all) and sprinkle with sesame seeds (if using). Bake until puffed and golden brown, 22 to 26 minutes. Serve.

Mushroom Pinwheels

—⟶⟶⟶—

Makes *about 28 pinwheels*

—⟶⟶⟶—

1 pound CREMINI
MUSHROOMS, trimmed

2 tablespoons UNSALTED
BUTTER

2 medium SHALLOTS, minced

1½ teaspoons KOSHER SALT

1 tablespoon minced FRESH
THYME

2 GARLIC CLOVES, minced

½ teaspoon FRESHLY GROUND
BLACK PEPPER

¼ cup MADEIRA

1 (14-ounce) package PUFF
PASTRY, thawed

3 tablespoons UNSEASONED
PANKO BREAD CRUMBS

1 large EGG, lightly beaten

BRIANNA AND ROGER MAC steal away for a moment of silence and solitude amid the revelries of Jocasta and Duncan's wedding dinner, but not without first procuring a tray of savories and goblets of wine ("The Lists of Venus," *The Fiery Cross*). Our rendition of the mushroom pasty that Bree relishes features a duxelle (sautéed minced mushrooms) accented with earthy thyme and sweet sautéed shallots, finished with heady Madeira (though you can swap in sherry, port, or Marsala with delicious results), and rolled up in buttery pastry. Cremini mushrooms have superior depth of flavor and are widely available at most grocery stores, but regular white button mushrooms will also do. When pulsing the mushrooms in the food processor, be careful not to fully pulverize them, which turns them into a watery mush. Rather, chop them so the pieces are about the size of peas. A sprinkling of panko on top of the mushroom filling helps prevent the inner layers of the pinwheel from getting soggy and aids browning in the oven. Something with sherry or a sherry-finished whisky would be just the thing with these umami-rich pastries—try the Chess and Conversation on page 96.

✦

1. Add the mushrooms to the bowl of a food processor and pulse until finely chopped, 8 to 12 pulses, scraping down the bowl and redistributing the mushrooms halfway through. (Do not overprocess; if any large pieces remain after 12 pulses, remove them and chop by hand.) Melt the butter in a 12-inch skillet over medium-low heat. Add the shallots and ½ teaspoon of the salt and cook, stirring occasionally, until the shallots start to brown around the edges, 6 to 9 minutes. Add the thyme, garlic, and pepper and cook, stirring, until fragrant, 1 to 2 minutes. Add the mushrooms and the remaining 1 teaspoon of salt, increase the heat to medium-high, and cook,

Recipe Continues

NOTE: *Chilling the filled dough, while not completely necessary, helps yield thinner slices, thus crispier pastry.*

stirring frequently and redistributing into an even layer, until the liquid has evaporated and the mixture begins to brown and form a layer on the bottom of the pan, 12 to 16 minutes. Add the Madeira and bring to a simmer, scraping up any browned bits from the bottom of the pan, then cook until the liquid has evaporated, 1 to 3 minutes. Remove the pan from the heat, spread the filling into an even layer, and let cool.

2. Line two rimmed baking sheets with parchment paper. On a lightly floured counter, roll the puff pastry into a 12 by 15-inch rectangle with the long side parallel to the edge of the counter. Transfer the mushroom mixture to the pastry and spread into an even layer, leaving a ½-inch border along the top, then sprinkle the filling evenly with the panko. Brush the top ½ inch of exposed pastry with the egg. Starting at the bottom long edge, roll the dough into a tight cylinder. Transfer the cylinder seam side down to one of the prepared baking sheets and refrigerate until firm, at least 30 minutes and up to 3 hours (see note).

3. Place oven racks in the upper- and lower-middle positions and heat the oven to 425°F. Slide the chilled log onto a cutting board, reserving the baking sheet. Use a sharp serrated knife to slice the log into scant ½-inch disks, turning the log as you go and reshaping the disks as needed. Transfer to the prepared baking sheets, spacing them evenly apart. Brush the tops of the disks with egg wash (you might not use it all), then transfer to the prepared racks and bake until golden brown, 24 to 28 minutes, switching and rotating the pans halfway through. Serve warm or at room temperature.

Crispy Fish Cakes

WITH
SAFFRON AIOLI

—⁓⁓⁓—

Makes *about 22 fish cakes*

—⁓⁓⁓—

1 large EGG plus 1 large YOLK

2 tablespoons MAYONNAISE

1 teaspoon finely grated
LEMON ZEST

½ teaspoon FRESHLY GROUND
BLACK PEPPER

1 pound SKINLESS WHITE
FISH FILLETS
(such as cod, haddock, or hake),
cut into 1-inch pieces

1½ teaspoons KOSHER SALT

1 cup UNSEASONED PANKO
BREAD CRUMBS

3 tablespoons minced FRESH
PARSLEY

1 tablespoon FRESHLY
SQUEEZED LEMON JUICE

IN THE EIGHTEENTH century as much as the twenty-first, saffron was a precious commodity. When Geilie brings some of the crimson threads to Mrs. Fitz to prepare for the duke, it's clear that the cook is going to the greatest lengths of extravagance ("By the Pricking of My Thumbs," *Outlander*). Even today most saffron, which is the stigma of a flower in the crocus family, is hand-picked and imported from the Middle East. Thankfully, it's widely available at grocery and specialty stores and doesn't require a pop-in from a devious time traveler to acquire. To really showcase the brilliant color and slightly bitter, floral flavor of the spice, we let it take center stage in an aioli to serve with simple fried fish cakes. If you've never made your own aioli or mayonnaise, don't be intimidated; just be patient and start adding the oil as slowly as possible, drop by drop, then pour quicker as the mixture emulsifies. You can use any neutral oil for frying (vegetable, peanut, safflower), but canola has a cleaner taste for aioli. You'll need about 1 cup of oil for frying the fish cakes, but the exact volume will depend on the size and shape of your skillet. You can't go wrong part-nering lemon with fish, and that holds true when picking a drink as well; shake up the Pink Linen Gown on page 58.

❖

1. Line a rimmed baking sheet with parchment paper. In a large bowl, whisk the whole egg, mayonnaise, lemon zest, and pepper until smooth. Add the fish to the bowl of a food processor, sprinkle with 1 teaspoon of the salt, and pulse until very finely chopped, 8 to 10 pulses. Transfer to the bowl with the egg mixture along with ⅓ cup of the panko and the parsley and fold until thoroughly combined. Using damp hands and working with a scant 2 tablespoons of the fish mixture at a time, form 2-inch patties. Transfer the fish patties to the prepared baking sheet. Refrigerate until firm, at least 20 minutes.

Recipe Continues

1 small GARLIC CLOVE,
finely grated

Pinch of SAFFRON

⅔ cup CANOLA OIL,
plus more for frying

LEMON WEDGES
for serving

2. Meanwhile, combine the lemon juice, garlic, ¼ teaspoon of the salt, and the saffron in a medium bowl and let sit for 15 minutes. Add the egg yolk and whisk until evenly combined. Whisking constantly, slowly drizzle in the ⅔ cup of oil starting with just a few drops at a time and pouring faster as the mixture emulsifies; set aside.

3. Combine the remaining ⅔ cup of panko and the remaining ¼ teaspoon of salt in a shallow bowl. Set a wire rack inside a second rimmed baking sheet. Add enough oil to a 12-inch skillet to measure ¼ inch deep and heat over medium-high heat until just smoking and an instant read thermometer registers 375°F (this could take 5 to 10 minutes depending on your stovetop). Working with a few patties at a time, transfer to the panko mixture and gently press to coat both sides. Transfer to the hot oil, then continue coating the cakes and adding them to the pan (you should be able to fit about half of the cakes). Fry until golden brown, 2 to 4 minutes per side, adjusting the heat as necessary if the crumbs begin to brown too quickly and transferring the cakes to the prepared rack as they finish cooking. Repeat with the remaining patties, returning the oil to 375°F between batches, if necessary. Serve with lemon wedges and saffron aioli. (To make ahead, transfer the baking sheet and wire rack with the fried cakes to a 200°F oven and keep warm for up to 1 hour.)

Sweet Potato Biscuits

———

Makes *about twenty
2-inch biscuits*

———

1 pound SWEET POTATOES
(2 to 4 small to medium)

1¾ cups (8¾ ounces)
ALL-PURPOSE FLOUR,
plus more for the counter

2 tablespoons PACKED LIGHT
BROWN SUGAR

2½ teaspoons BAKING POWDER

¾ teaspoon FINE-GRAIN
SEA SALT or table salt

½ teaspoon SMOKED PAPRIKA
(optional)

¼ teaspoon BAKING SODA

8 tablespoons (1 stick)
UNSALTED BUTTER,
cut into ½-inch cubes and
chilled, plus 1 tablespoon
melted unsalted butter

COMPOUND BUTTER (see note),
COUNTRY HAM, and
SPICY MUSTARD for serving
(optional)

WHILE WE CAN only imagine that the yams Claire, Jamie, and the gang roasted in the campfire while building their homestead in "Hearth Blessing" (*Drums of Autumn*) took on a pleasantly smoky aroma, we're also certain that these flaky little biscuits are a fair bit more appetizing. While optional, a touch of smoked paprika pays homage to that faraway campfire. For those without microwaves, pierce the potatoes as instructed, then bake them in a 450°F oven until tender, about 1 hour. If you don't have a food processor, you can whisk the dry ingredients together and use a pastry cutter or two knives to cut the butter into the flour mixture by hand. You can reroll the scraps once after stamping out the first round of biscuits, but any more than that and you risk toughening the dough. The biscuits are lovely as is or with a smear of salted butter, but we also love them spread with mustard and piled with salty ham. (If you're serving them with true country ham, decrease the salt in the biscuits to ½ teaspoon.) When it comes to a beverage, pair like with like, opting for something smoky like the Peat's Dragon on page 85, which is extra sultry thanks to both Scotch and mezcal.

———✦———

1. Prick the potatoes all over with a fork, transfer to a plate, and microwave on high until tender, 12 to 16 minutes, flipping twice during cooking. Immediately cut open to release the steam and let cool. When cool enough to handle, scoop the flesh into a large bowl and mash it thoroughly with a fork. Measure the mashed potato and discard anything in excess of 1 cup. Transfer to the refrigerator and chill until cool to the touch, at least 20 minutes.

Recipe Continues

NOTE: *For a quick compound butter, blitz a stick of softened, unsalted butter in the food processor with ½ cup of chopped fresh herbs such as chives, parsley, and dill until evenly combined. Roll the butter up in a sheet of parchment paper in the shape of a log and chill until firm.*

2. Place an oven rack in the upper-middle position, heat the oven to 425°F, and line a rimmed baking sheet with parchment paper. In the bowl of a food processor, combine the flour, brown sugar, baking powder, salt, paprika (if using), and baking soda and process until combined, 15 to 30 seconds. Add the chilled butter and pulse until coarsely ground, 6 to 8 pulses. Add the flour mixture to the bowl with the sweet potato and stir gently until just combined (do not overmix). Transfer the dough to a lightly floured counter and pat into a 7-inch circle about ¾ inch thick. Use a 1¾-inch biscuit cutter to stamp out rounds and transfer to the prepared baking sheet, spacing them evenly apart. Brush the tops of the biscuits with the melted butter and bake until golden brown, 12 to 16 minutes, rotating the pan halfway through. Let cool for at least 10 minutes before splitting, filling with the butter, ham, and spicy mustard, if desired, and serving.

Watercress Pesto Chicken Salad
IN ENDIVE

Makes about 30 endive cups

2 bone-in, skin-on
CHICKEN BREASTS
(about 1½ pounds total)

1 tablespoon plus ⅓ cup
EXTRA-VIRGIN OLIVE OIL

2¼ teaspoons KOSHER SALT

1 bunch WATERCRESS,
stemmed (about 3 cups lightly
packed, or substitute 3 ounces
baby arugula)

2 teaspoons finely grated
LEMON ZEST

1 GARLIC CLOVE, chopped

1 ounce PARMESAN CHEESE,
finely grated (about ½ cup, see
headnote on page 217)

WE MAY NOT have the looming threat of scurvy to compel us to eat watercress ("The Wanderer," *Voyager*), and when it's blitzed into a bright pesto alongside nutty Parmesan, tart lemon, and fruity olive oil, we don't need it. Combined with juicy chunks of chicken, it makes for a superb salad, and while roasting bone-in breasts ensures succulent meat, you can always substitute 2 cups of chopped skinless, boneless rotisserie chicken. Watercress is often available bunched in the produce section alongside the lettuce but is also sold with the roots still intact as hydroponic "land" or "upland" cress and sometimes even prewashed and bagged. All versions will do, and baby arugula makes an excellent stand-in if you can't find any. Instead of pureeing nuts into the sauce as is traditional with pesto, we chose to add textural interest with toasted, chopped pistachios. You want the chicken to be warm when you toss it with the pesto, but the salad (sans pistachios) can be refrigerated for a day before assembling the endive cups. Stir in the nuts right before serving to preserve their crunch. Pair green with green when it comes to libations and make the Consolation Cup on page 179.

---

1. Place an oven rack in the middle position and heat the oven to 375°F. Place the chicken breasts on a small, rimmed baking sheet or oven-safe skillet and use your hands to coat evenly with 1 tablespoon of the oil and 1 teaspoon of the salt. Roast, skin side up, until cooked through and the thickest part of the breast registers 160°F on an instant read thermometer, 30 to 35 minutes.

Recipe Continues

1 tablespoon FRESHLY
SQUEEZED LEMON JUICE

⅓ cup PISTACHIOS, toasted and
coarsely chopped (see note)

3 BELGIAN ENDIVES,
trimmed, leaves separated

2. Meanwhile, combine the watercress, lemon zest, garlic, and remaining 1¼ teaspoons of salt in the bowl of a food processor and pulse until finely chopped, 6 to 8 pulses. With the motor running, drizzle in the remaining ⅓ cup of oil until fully incorporated. Add the Parmesan and lemon juice and pulse until just combined, 2 to 4 pulses. Scrape the pesto into a medium bowl and set aside.

3. When the chicken is cool enough to handle, remove and discard the skin and bones and chop the meat into ½-inch pieces. Add the chicken and the pistachios to the pesto and fold until evenly coated. Spoon the chicken salad into the endive leaves and serve.

NOTE: *While you're welcome to shell and toast your own pistachios, Wonderful sells bags of shelled, roasted, and lightly salted nuts that are delicious and using them in this recipe saves time.*

Warm Spinach Dip

Serves 4 to 6

1 (16-ounce) bag frozen
WHOLE-LEAF SPINACH,
thawed

1 tablespoon EXTRA-VIRGIN
OLIVE OIL

6 SCALLIONS, thinly sliced,
white and green parts separated

2 GARLIC CLOVES, minced

8 ounces CREAM CHEESE,
softened and cut into 8 pieces

3 ounces PARMESAN CHEESE,
finely grated (about 1½ cups;
see headnote)

1 cup (8 ounces) WHOLE-MILK
PLAIN GREEK YOGURT

3 ounces GRUYÈRE CHEESE,
shredded (about 1 cup)

2 teaspoons finely grated
LEMON ZEST

2 teaspoons VINEGAR-BASED
HOT SAUCE, plus more for
serving (optional)

ROGER'S CHILDHOOD IMAGININGS conjured a dragon that breathed green fire because it ate nothing but spinach ("The Plot Thickens," *Dragonfly in Amber*), but we preferred to dream up a bubbling, melty, decadent dip featuring the verdant leaves. Chopped spinach will work here, but we favored the texture of frozen whole-leaf. You can thaw the spinach in the refrigerator overnight, on the counter for a few hours, or in the microwave. For the best texture, grate the Parmesan on a rasp-style grater like a Microplane or on the smallest holes of your box grater; if you use pre-grated store-bought Parmesan, the volume will be about half what we list here (but the weight will be the same). We love the tang of yogurt to balance the richness of this dip, but sour cream will also work. And while Gruyère is our top choice, any good melting cheese like mozzarella or fontina will do just fine (use the large holes of your box grater for this cheese). It may seem like a meager amount, but don't skip the nutmeg! It's an homage to the best steakhouse creamed spinach and really does make a difference. The dip can be made ahead and refrigerated in the baking dish for up to 2 days. If making ahead, let the dip come to room temperature before baking and increase the baking time to about 30 minutes. You can make the toasts as instructed in the recipe for Crab and Chile Crostini on page 228, omitting the mustard and lemon zest, for scooping, or opt for the ease of bagged pita chips. Something light and slightly fruity is welcome alongside this rich, cheesy number; we suggest the Holiday Clove Spritz on page 152.

1. Place an oven rack in the upper-middle position and heat the oven to 400°F. Place the spinach in the center of a clean kitchen towel, gather the corners together, and wring out as much liquid as possible. Heat the oil in a 12-inch skillet over medium heat until shimmering. Add the scallion whites and

Recipe Continues

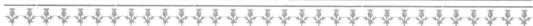

½ teaspoon FRESHLY GRATED NUTMEG

½ teaspoon FRESHLY GROUND BLACK PEPPER

PITA CHIPS, TOASTED BAGUETTE SLICES, or STURDY CRACKERS for serving

garlic and cook, stirring frequently, until the garlic is browned around the edges, 2 to 4 minutes. Add the spinach and stir until heated through and evenly combined, 1 to 2 minutes. Decrease the heat to low, add the cream cheese, and stir until completely melted; remove the pan from the heat.

2. Stir 1 cup of the Parmesan, the yogurt, Gruyère, scallion greens, lemon zest, hot sauce (if using), nutmeg, and pepper into the spinach mixture until evenly combined. Transfer to a 2-quart baking dish, scraping out the pan, and smooth into an even layer. Sprinkle with the remaining ½ cup of Parmesan and bake until bubbling around the edges, about 20 minutes. Leaving the dish on the upper-middle rack, heat the broiler to high and broil the dip until browned on top, about 5 minutes. Serve with pita chips, baguette slices, or crackers and more hot sauce, if desired.

Crispy Polenta

WITH

TURNIP-APPLE-BACON SLAW

—⁓⁓⁓—

𝕸akes *16 to 20 polenta rounds*

—⁓⁓⁓—

1 (16-ounce) tube
PREPARED POLENTA

3 tablespoons EXTRA-VIRGIN
OLIVE OIL

4 strips BACON, cut crosswise
into ¼-inch slices

3 tablespoons APPLE CIDER
VINEGAR

1 tablespoon WHOLE-GRAIN
MUSTARD

2 teaspoons PACKED
BROWN SUGAR

¾ teaspoon KOSHER SALT

½ teaspoon FRESHLY GROUND
BLACK PEPPER

CORNMEAL MUSH, LIKE the one served to the hunting party in "Wildfire" from *The Fiery Cross*, may not whet the appetite, but how about crisp-chewy oven-fried rounds of polenta? You can use store-bought polenta for convenience, but feel free to make your own. Pair these with a tangy slaw of raw julienned turnips and apples laced with grainy mustard and sharp tarragon, all united by a backbone of meaty sautéed bacon. You can use a mandoline to cut the turnip and apple, but a sharp knife and a little patience will also do the trick. Start by slicing a thin sliver off one side of the turnip, giving yourself a flat surface instead of a rounded one. Rest it on the flat side and slice the turnip as thinly as possible (aim for about ⅛ inch), then stack the slices a few at a time and slice again, creating ⅛-inch matchsticks. Repeat this technique with the apple, cutting around the core and discarding the seeds and stem as you go. The slightly anise-y flavor of tarragon really pops in the slaw, but feel free to use parsley instead. It may seem like a surfeit of oil when coating the polenta, but it's key to prevent sticking and achieving a crisp crust (and still much less than you'd use to pan-fry!). An ale or a Scotch-based cocktail is welcome alongside a tray of these, complementing the mustardy, smoky dressing.

❖

1. Place an oven rack in the lower-middle position and heat the oven to 475°F. Slice the polenta into scant ½-inch rounds and pat dry. Spread the polenta rounds on a rimmed baking sheet and drizzle evenly with 1½ tablespoons of the oil. Flip each round and repeat with the remaining 1½ tablespoons of oil, using your hands to make sure each round is thoroughly coated, then flip again. Bake until golden and crisp on the bottom, 25 to 30 minutes, rotating the pan halfway through. (If the polenta sticks to the pan, return to the oven until it easily releases.) Use a thin metal spatula to transfer the polenta to a clean kitchen towel, browned side up, and set aside.

Recipe Continues

1 medium TURNIP
(about 6 ounces), peeled and
cut into matchsticks

1 GRANNY SMITH APPLE,
cored and cut into matchsticks

1 tablespoon chopped
FRESH TARRAGON

2. Meanwhile, line a plate with a double layer of paper towels. Add the bacon to a 10-inch skillet, place over medium-low heat, and cook, stirring often, until the fat has rendered and the bacon is browned, 7 to 9 minutes. Slide the pan off the heat and use a slotted spoon to transfer the bacon to the prepared plate, then pour off all but 2 tablespoons of the fat. Add the vinegar, mustard, sugar, salt, and pepper to the remaining fat in the pan and bring to a simmer over medium heat. Cook, whisking and scraping up any browned bits from the bottom of the pan, until slightly thickened, 1 to 3 minutes; remove the pan from the heat.

3. Transfer the polenta rounds to a serving platter or board, browned side up. In a large bowl, toss the turnip, apple, and tarragon with the dressing until evenly coated. Stir in the reserved bacon, then divide the slaw evenly among the polenta rounds and serve immediately.

Prosciutto-Wrapped Figs

WITH
BLUE CHEESE
AND WALNUTS

—◦◦◦◦◦—

Makes *about 12 fig bites*

—◦◦◦◦◦—

¼ cup WALNUT HALVES

½ cup BALSAMIC VINEGAR

3 ounces thinly sliced
PROSCIUTTO

12 FRESH FIGS (2 pints),
stemmed

2 ounces BLUE CHEESE,
cut into 12 pieces

1 teaspoon FRESHLY CRACKED
BLACK PEPPER

FIGS WERE NOT only a culinary delicacy but a boon to intestinal health, and while sea journeys like Claire's aboard the *Porpoise* ("We Meet a Porpoise," *Voyager*) necessitated the purser, Mr. Overholt, to stock the dried version, seasonal plump, fresh figs are put to good use here. Either black Mission or brown Turkish figs will work, but larger fruit is better (there should be about 6 to a pint), and you want them ripe but firm. The earthiness and crunch of toasted nuts (use pecans or almonds if you prefer) stands out against the tender flesh of the fruit, and a good-quality sharp blue cheese (Stilton is a good option, but Francophiles may favor Roquefort) will warm and soften while baking but not melt and ooze out of the fig. You want the heat of the oven to render the prosciutto crisp but not shatteringly so—it should still have a pleasant chew to it. And if you have balsamic glaze or reduction in your pantry, feel free to use that, skipping the simmering in step 1. Blue cheese and port are a classic pairing for good reason—try the Ruby Port and a Fine Cheroot on page 86.

———————◆———————

1. Place an oven rack in the middle position and heat the oven to 400°F. Toast the walnuts in a dry 8-inch skillet over medium-low heat until fragrant and spotty brown, 3 to 5 minutes. Transfer to a plate, reserving the skillet. Add the vinegar to the skillet, bring to a simmer over medium heat, and cook until small, foamy bubbles appear on the surface and the liquid appears thickened but not syrupy, 6 to 8 minutes. Remove the pan from the heat and let cool.

2. Cut the prosciutto lengthwise into halves or thirds, depending on the size of your slices, to make rough 1½-inch strips. Working with one fig at a time, cut a slit down the side from top to bottom and gently fan open. Place a piece of cheese and a walnut half inside and press closed. Wrap the fig in 1 or 2 pieces of prosciutto, doing your best to cover the slit and any exposed cheese, and secure with a toothpick. Transfer

to a rimmed baking sheet and repeat with the remaining figs, cheese, walnuts, and prosciutto. Bake until the prosciutto is crisp and the figs are warmed through, 12 to 16 minutes. Transfer to a platter, drizzle with the balsamic reduction, sprinkle with the pepper, and serve.

Smoked Salmon

AND

FRIED CAPERS *ON* CUCUMBER ROUNDS

—————

Makes *about 32 cucumber rounds*

—————

8 ounces CREAM CHEESE, cut into 8 pieces and softened

4 ounces SMOKED SALMON, roughly chopped

2 tablespoons chopped FRESH DILL, plus fronds for serving

1 to 2 tablespoons SCOTCH WHISKY

2 teaspoons finely grated LEMON ZEST plus 1 tablespoon FRESHLY SQUEEZED LEMON JUICE

1 teaspoon DIJON MUSTARD

3 tablespoons CANOLA or olive OIL

3 tablespoons drained CAPERS, well dried

1 ENGLISH CUCUMBER, trimmed and cut into ¼-inch rounds

AS A NOD TO the many mentions of smoked fish and pickled herring in the *Outlander* books, this easy yet impressive smoked salmon puree gets an extra hit of smoke (and Scottish cred) from the addition of Scotch whisky. To accommodate varying levels of smokiness in your whisky, start with 1 tablespoon, then taste and go from there. Choose Scottish smoked salmon to really drive home the point, but any good-quality smoked salmon or nova will do. Cream cheese makes the perfect neutral base, and the classic flavors of dill, mustard, and lemon bolster the fish without overpowering it. Use vinegar-brined, not salt-packed, capers for this recipe, and to minimize splattering while frying, gently press and pat them dry with paper towels. Since it's a quick fry, the oil doesn't degrade and actually takes on a lovely flavor from the capers— let it cool and whisk it into a vinaigrette for a simple salad. If you can't find English cucumbers, peel a standard cucumber before cutting it into rounds. The salmon mixture can also be smeared on toast points or layered into finger sandwiches. To accentuate the classic elegance of these morsels, choose something simple and refreshing like the Appellation Cooler on page 162.

———————— ✦ ————————

1. In the bowl of a food processor, combine the cream cheese, salmon, dill, whisky, lemon zest and juice, and mustard and process until smooth, 30 to 60 seconds, scraping down the bowl halfway through. Transfer the mixture to a piping bag fitted with a star tip. (The puree can be refrigerated for up to 1 day; allow to come to room temperature before serving.)

2. Line a plate with a double layer of paper towels. Heat the oil in an 8-inch skillet over medium-high heat until just smoking. Carefully add the capers and cook, swirling the pan, until crisp and browned, 2 to 4 minutes. Use a slotted spoon or fish spatula to transfer the capers to the prepared plate. Pipe the mousse onto the cucumber rounds, then top with a few capers and a dill frond and serve.

Sharp Cheddar Fricos

WITH

RAISIN CHUTNEY

—◦◦◦◦◦◦—

Makes *about 40 crisps*

—◦◦◦◦◦◦—

2 teaspoons OLIVE OIL

2 medium SHALLOTS, minced

½ teaspoon KOSHER SALT

1½ teaspoons finely grated
FRESH GINGER

¼ teaspoon FRESHLY GROUND
BLACK PEPPER

½ cup RAISINS

½ cup WATER

¼ cup APPLE CIDER VINEGAR

3 tablespoons PACKED BROWN
SUGAR

1 tablespoon ARMAGNAC or
BRANDY (optional)

3 ounces EXTRA-SHARP
CHEDDAR CHEESE, grated
(about 1½ cups)

THROUGHOUT *THE FIERY CROSS*, there are several mentions of raisin pie and tart, usually baked by Mrs. Bug and enjoyed with tea or a dollop of clotted cream. For our take on a sticky, dried fruit concoction, we chose to lean into the savory side, spiking our raisin chutney with shallots, black pepper, and a generous glug of cider vinegar as well as fresh ginger and molasses-y brown sugar. While optional, a hit of brandy rounds out the flavors. The technique of transforming grated cheese into a salty, waferlike crisp, also known as a frico, is more often seen with harder cheeses like Parmesan, but an aged extra-sharp Cheddar works beautifully. The fricos will be soft when they first come out of the oven but should look browned throughout, not just around the edges, and smell toasty; they'll quickly firm up as they cool. The chutney and fricos can both be made a few hours in advance (or days in the case of the chutney), but assemble them right before serving. These bites are begging to be eaten alongside a cider-based cocktail such as the To the Core on page 147.

———————◆———————

1. Heat the oil in a small saucepan over medium-low heat until shimmering. Add the shallots and salt and cook, stirring often, until just beginning to brown, 3 to 5 minutes. Add the ginger and pepper and cook, stirring, until fragrant, about 30 seconds. Add the raisins, water, vinegar, sugar, and Armagnac (if using), increase the heat to medium-high, and bring to a simmer. Cook until thickened and syrupy, 8 to 12 minutes, stirring occasionally and adjusting the heat as necessary to maintain a lively simmer. Remove from the heat and let cool to room temperature. (Cooled chutney can be refrigerated for up to 3 days; allow to come to room temperature before proceeding with the recipe.)

2. Place oven racks in the upper- and lower-middle positions and heat the oven to 400°F. Line two baking sheets with parchment paper or silicone baking mats. Pinch up scant

2-teaspoon portions of the cheese and mound on the prepared pans, spacing at least 1½ inches apart. Bake until evenly golden, 8 to 12 minutes, switching and rotating the pans halfway through. Let the fricos cool for at least 5 minutes on the baking sheet, then use a thin metal spatula to transfer to a serving platter. Top each frico with a teaspoon of chutney and serve immediately.

Crab and Chile Crostini

— ✦ —

Makes *16 crostini*

— ✦ —

16 (½-inch) BAGUETTE SLICES

3 tablespoons EXTRA-VIRGIN
OLIVE OIL

2 teaspoons finely grated
LEMON ZEST

3 teaspoons DIJON MUSTARD

¼ teaspoon FRESHLY GROUND
BLACK PEPPER

2 tablespoons MAYONNAISE

1 tablespoon FRESHLY
SQUEEZED LEMON JUICE

8 ounces FRESH LUMP
CRABMEAT

1 small FRESNO CHILE,
stemmed and very thinly sliced
(seeded for less heat)

CELERY LEAVES, LEMON
WEDGES, and FLAKY SEA
SALT such as Maldon for serving

WHEN CLAIRE AND Jamie are invited to dinner at the Lillingtons' ("Great Prospects Fraught with Peril," *Drums of Autumn*), Claire notes a bountiful seafood platter with, among other things, "a vast quantity of tiny spiced crabs." We decided to skip the lavish display and focus on the winning combination of sweet, succulent crabmeat and a spicy kick of heat, here courtesy of a fresh Fresno chile. While a fresh baguette will work, making the toasts, or crostini, for the crab is a great way to use up stale bread. Mustard does double duty in this recipe, flavoring both the bread and the crab mixture, and just a touch of mayo holds the topping together. In lieu of a Fresno chile, turn to a jalapeño or serrano. The celery leaves, utilized here like an herb, aren't obligatory, but their grassy, slightly bitter flavor is a welcome touch, and the sea salt echoes the salinity of the crustacean beautifully. The toasts and crab mixture can both be made several hours in advance (refrigerate the crab) but should not be combined until right before serving. A delicate, bubbly cocktail with a bit of sweetness to counteract the spice is best with these; try Dr. Stern's Prescription on page 176.

— ✦ —

1. Place an oven rack in the middle position and heat the oven to 400°F. Arrange the baguette slices in a single layer on a rimmed baking sheet. In a small bowl, combine the oil, lemon zest, 2 teaspoons of the mustard, and the black pepper. Brush one side of the baguette slices evenly with the oil mixture and bake until crisp and golden brown around the edges, 12 to 14 minutes; let cool slightly.

2. In a medium bowl, combine the mayonnaise, lemon juice, and remaining 1 teaspoon of mustard, then gently fold in the crab and chile. Divide the crab mixture evenly among the baguette slices and sprinkle with celery leaves. Right before serving, squeeze a lemon wedge over the top and sprinkle with flaky sea salt.

Sweet Corn Cakes

WITH

APRICOTS *AND* CHERRIES

Makes *12 cakes*

3 tablespoons plus ¾ cup SUGAR

3 FRESH APRICOTS, each cut into 8 wedges

12 FRESH CHERRIES, stemmed and pitted

¾ cup ALL-PURPOSE FLOUR

⅓ cup CORNMEAL

1 teaspoon BAKING POWDER

¼ teaspoon BAKING SODA

¼ teaspoon FINE-GRAIN SEA SALT or table salt

1 large EGG plus 1 large YOLK

½ cup (1 stick) UNSALTED BUTTER, melted

½ cup SOUR CREAM

1 tablespoon KIRSCH

½ teaspoon VANILLA EXTRACT

WHEN PREPARING FOR THE GATHERING at Castle Leoch, Claire helps by accompanying the young women of the castle to the orchards outside the walls to pick "bright cherries and smooth, plump apricots . . . dropping them into our baskets in juicy heaps" ("The Gathering," *Outlander*). The two fruits showcased here are enrobed in a buttery batter enriched with sour cream and cornmeal. Baking spray (like PAM for baking, which includes flour) is ideal for coating the muffin cups, but you can also melt extra butter and brush it on with a pastry brush. Just be thorough to prevent sticking! While apricots are ideal for their size, small peaches, nectarines, or plums will also work, and if fresh cherries aren't in season, substitute the frozen pitted ones, halving and only using one-half per cake if large. The kirsch brings home the fruit flavor of these rustic little cakes, but apricot brandy would be just as good. After melting the butter, don't let it cool too much before whisking it into the sugar and eggs, otherwise the batter may be too thick to easily scoop into the muffin tin. Set a timer for cooling the cakes in the pan—any longer than 5 minutes before turning out and they may begin to stick. They're best eaten slightly warm or at room temperature and make a perfect accompaniment to afternoon tea, while the addition of lightly sweetened whipped cream (add a glug of kirsch to that, too) or a scoop of vanilla ice cream makes them a company-worthy dessert. Pair with an Up the Hudson on page 75 or the Bonnie Prince's Consolation on page 104.

* ❖ *

1. Place an oven rack in the lower-middle position and heat the oven to 350°F. Thoroughly spray the cups of a 12-cup muffin pan with baking spray, then sprinkle ¾ teaspoon of the sugar in the bottom of each cup, tapping and rotating the pan to evenly coat the bottom and lower perimeter of the cups. Place 2 apricot wedges and 1 cherry in the bottom of each cup; set aside.

Recipe Continues

NOTE: *These cakes are not supposed to rise like muffins—you actually want the "tops" fairly flat since they're served fruit side up.*

2. In a small bowl, whisk the flour, cornmeal, baking powder, baking soda, and salt until evenly combined. In a medium bowl, vigorously whisk the remaining ¾ cup of sugar and the egg and yolk until lightened. Whisking constantly, slowly add the butter and whisk until emulsified. Whisk in the sour cream, kirsch, and vanilla. Add the flour mixture and whisk until no lumps remain.

3. Use a ¼-cup dry measuring cup to scoop the batter over the fruit in the muffin tin, dividing evenly between the cups and making sure to completely cover the fruit. Bake until the cakes are browned around the edges and the centers spring back when gently pressed, 18 to 22 minutes, rotating the pan halfway through (see note). Let the cakes cool in the pan for 5 minutes, then invert onto a wire rack and let cool for at least 10 minutes. Serve warm or at room temperature.

Chocolate Almond Shortbread

—〰〰—

𝔐𝔞𝔨𝔢𝔰 *32 cookies*

—〰〰—

1 cup SLIVERED ALMONDS

1½ cups ALL-PURPOSE FLOUR

¾ cup EXTRA-FINE ALMOND FLOUR

¼ teaspoon FINE-GRAIN SEA SALT or table salt

1 cup (2 sticks) UNSALTED BUTTER, at room temperature

¾ cup SUGAR

¾ teaspoon ALMOND EXTRACT

4 ounces SEMISWEET CHOCOLATE, finely chopped

2 teaspoons COCONUT OIL

I N "THE SOUNDS OF SILENCE" (*The Fiery Cross*), Bree recounts a dream where her craving for a Hershey's bar with almonds is magically fulfilled; she smells the chocolate as she unfolds the paper wrapper. All due respect to Hershey's and milk chocolate, but we'll take the aroma of these rich, buttery almond cookies wafting from the oven and the bittersweet bite of dark chocolate any day. Blanched, slivered almonds provide a meatier texture in these cookies as opposed to delicate sliced almonds, but the latter will work just fine. Look for almond flour made with blanched, not skin on, almonds—Bob's Red Mill makes one. While moving the cookies to a wire rack just to return them to the baking sheet before drizzling with chocolate may seem fussy, the air circulation allowed by the rack is essential to that classic crumbly yet dense shortbread texture. Pair them with something bitter and bracing, like the Sgian-Dubh on page 88.

———◆———

1. Toast the almonds in a dry, 10-inch skillet over medium-low heat, stirring and tossing frequently, until fragrant and spotty brown, 6 to 8 minutes. Remove the pan from the heat and let cool. In a medium bowl, whisk together the all-purpose flour, almond flour, and salt until combined. In the bowl of a stand mixer fitted with the paddle attachment, beat the butter and sugar on medium speed until light and fluffy, 2 to 4 minutes. Scrape down the bowl, add the almond extract, and beat until incorporated, about 30 seconds. Add the flour mixture and beat on low speed until fully incorporated, 1 to 2 minutes, scraping down the bowl and the beater halfway through. Add the almonds and mix until evenly distributed. Transfer the dough to a clean surface and knead gently to ensure that all of the ingredients are evenly distributed. Divide the dough in half and use a sheet of parchment paper to form each half into an 8-inch log about 1¾ inches in diameter. Refrigerate for at least 1 hour and up to 3 days.

Recipe Continues

2. Heat the oven to 350°F and line two rimmed baking sheets with parchment paper or silicone baking mats. Working with one log at a time, use a serrated knife to slice the dough into scant ½-inch-thick rounds, using a sawing motion and rotating the dough between cuts. Transfer to one of the prepared pans, spacing the rounds evenly apart, and bake until the surface looks dry and the edges are just beginning to color, 13 to 15 minutes. Let cool on the baking sheet for 5 minutes, then transfer to a wire rack and let cool completely, reserving the lined baking sheet. Repeat with the second dough log.

3. Combine the chocolate and coconut oil in a small, heatproof bowl and set over a small saucepan of barely simmering water until just melted, stirring frequently. Return the cookies to the reserved lined baking sheets, then use a spoon or small spatula to drizzle with the chocolate mixture. Let sit until set, at least 2 hours.

INDEX

Copyright © 2024 by Diana Gabaldon
Photographs copyright © 2024 by Aimee Twigger

Published in the United States by Random House
Worlds, an imprint of Random House, a division of
Penguin Random House LLC, New York.
RandomHouseBooks.com

RANDOM HOUSE is a registered trademark, and
RANDOM HOUSE WORLDS and colophon
are trademarks of Penguin Random House LLC.

Library of Congress Cataloging-in-Publication Data
Names: Random House Worlds [Firm], publisher.
Title: Outlander cocktails: the official drinks guide inspired
    by the series.
Description: First edition. || New York: Random House
    Worlds, 2024. ||
Includes index.
Identifiers: LCCN 2023028563 [print] || LCCN
    2023028564 [ebook] || ISBN 9781984862396
    [hardcover] || ISBN 9781984862402 [ebook]
Subjects: LCSH: Cocktails. || Outlander [Television
    program]——Miscellanea. ||
LCGFT: Cookbooks
Classification: LCC TX951 .O98 2018 [print] || LCC TX951
    [ebook] ||
    DDC 641.87/4——dc23/eng/20230623
LC record available at https://lccn.loc.gov/2023028563
LC ebook record available at https://lccn.loc.
    gov/2023028564

Printed in China on acid-free paper

ACQUIRING EDITOR: Lindley Boegehold
PROJECT EDITOR: Kim Keller
PRODUCTION EDITOR: Kelly Chian
ART DIRECTOR: Jenny Davis
DESIGNER: Laura Palese
COMPOSITOR: Merri Ann Morrell
PRODUCTION MANAGER: Maggie Hart
COLOR SEPARATIONS: North Market Street Graphics
DRINKS AND PROP STYLIST: Suze Morrison
FOOD STYLIST: Aimee Twigger
PROP STYLIST: Ros Atkinson
PHOTO RETOUCHER: Ché Graham

RECIPE DEVELOPER, DRINKS: James Shy Freeman
RECIPE DEVELOPER, FOOD: Rebeccah Marsters
COPY EDITORS: Hope Clarke, Kristi Hein
PROOFREADERS: Maureen Clark, Melanie Gold,
Liana Faughnan, Megha Jain
INDEXER: Ina Gravitz

Design element credits:
Background photograph on page 10:
    SergeBertasiusPhotography/Shutterstock.com
Paper vintage background:
    Sk__Advance studio/Shutterstock.com
Green paper background:
    MM__photos/Shutterstock.com
Another paper background: P.siripak/Shutterstock.com
Cocktail illustration: sturgood/Shutterstock.com
Circular frame and corners used throughout:
    Pogaryts'kyy/Shutterstock.com
Thistle used in the crown/thistle icon throughout:
    Marta Leo/Shutterstock.com
Crown used in the crown/thistle icon throughout:
    Roberto Castillo/Shutterstock.com
Various borders used throughout:
    Vector Tradition/Shutterstock.com
Celtic icons used throughout:
    polosatik/Shutterstock.com
Additional Celtic icons used throughout:
    bomg/Shutterstock.com

9 8 7 6 5 4 3 2 1

First Edition